Jenny Alexander is a children's author who has written many books on real-life issues. Faced with the problem of bullying, she and her family looked for creative and effective ways of coping, and *When Your Child is Bullied* grew naturally out of that experience.

When Your Child
is Bullied

An Essential Guide
for Parents

Jenny Alexander

POCKET
BOOKS

LONDON • SYDNEY • NEW YORK • TORONTO

This edition first published in Great Britain by
Simon & Schuster UK Ltd, 2006
A CBS COMPANY

An earlier version of this book was published in 1998 as
Your Child: Bullying by Element Books Ltd.

1 3 5 7 9 10 8 6 4 2

Simon & Schuster UK Ltd
Africa House
64–78 Kingsway
London WC2B 6AH

www.simonsays.co.uk

Simon & Schuster Australia
Sydney

A CIP catalogue record for this book is available from the
British Library

ISBN 1-4165-2235-2
EAN 9 78141652235 5

Typeset in Garamond by M Rules
Printed and bound in Great Britain by
Cox & Wyman Ltd, Reading, Berks

Acknowledgements

I should like to thank everyone who has shared their bullying stories with me and all the authors whose work on so many different subjects has contributed to my understanding of the problem. I am particularly grateful to Susan Jeffers for giving me permission to use her 'pushing back your boundaries' idea and to Penny Parks for her 'inner child rescue scene'.

Contents

Conclusion: Your Powerful Child

Note: 'he' and 'she' have been used to describe your child in alternate chapters to avoid the more cumbersome 'he or she'. In the real-life scenarios, names have been changed to protect identities.

Introduction

I want to say at the outset that this is not a general book about bullying – it's a self-help book for parents whose children are being bullied. It doesn't contain facts and figures, statistics and psychological profiles, because its subject is the practical day-to-day challenge of helping your child to cope with bullying. I wrote it because if such a book had been available when my child was being bullied I think it could have saved my family from months of acute anxiety and pain.

Bullying is a shocking problem. First, there's the shock of finding out how cruel children can be to each other. Then, for parents, there's the shock of suddenly having to deal with a child under extreme stress and, finally, there's the shock of discovering that when your child is being bullied you become a victim too.

His unhappiness makes you unhappy; his fear makes you afraid. If he dreads going to school, you dread sending him. You feel the same impotent anger about the situation he's in and the same murderous hatred towards the people who are making him suffer. What's more, if you let yourself be overwhelmed by victim feelings it can become a vicious cycle, with your unhappiness making him even more miserable, and your worries making him even more anxious about going to school.

I didn't want my child to be a victim and I didn't want to be one either. So I wrote to all the anti-bullying organizations and ordered all the recommended books, looking for ideas about how to take effective action. I found that the conventional advice to parents fell into two main categories – what to ask your child's school to do and what to tell your child to do. There was absolutely nothing in terms of strategies parents could try at home, *with* their children.

As soon as my husband and I opened a dialogue with the school it occurred to me that even if they managed to stop the bullying our child would still be vulnerable. Children who have been bullied are likely to be bullied again simply because a precedent has been set. Children who are bullied repeatedly become less and less able to defend themselves. It was up to the school to sort out the current situation, but it was up to my child to learn how to stay safe.

However, most of the advice I found about what to tell a bullied child seemed to be either so obvious that he would already be doing it – such as avoiding the places where his tormentors hung out – or else completely impractical. It was only because I couldn't think what else to do that I suggested he tried it, and I certainly wished I hadn't.

It might sound fine in theory to say that bullied children should tell a teacher, pretend they don't care, practise walking tall, think of witty things to say, join clubs and make new friends but, as you will probably know if your child is being bullied, these are not real options for children whose self-esteem has taken a battering. Asking fragile children to do such things is setting them up for failure, and their failure will only make you feel more frustrated and helpless than ever.

I reached the conclusion that the conventional approach – trying to get bullied children to change their behaviour without first addressing their feelings – was putting the cart before the horse. It was pointless to ask children who felt bad about themselves to pretend they didn't, but if they felt good about themselves their behaviour would automatically change anyway. So how could you make a child feel good about himself? I didn't know, but I knew how to find out.

I went back to the bookshops and library, this time looking not for books on bullying, but for books on positive thinking, building self-esteem and coping with high levels of anger and fear.

These books, which I had never previously dreamed of reading, turned out to be packed with uplifting anecdotes, memorable quotations and practical exercises. I was sure the ideas in them could help my child, but they were all aimed at adults and I couldn't find anything similar written for children.

I decided to try the ideas out for myself. After all, I was a victim too. I had my own unhappiness, fear and anger about the bullying situation to deal with. If my child wanted to join in, he could, because I would explain what I was doing as I went along.

I started with positive thinking: it looked as if it would be easy and fun. I explained it to all of my children in terms of positive and negative words, and to illustrate the point I suggested we try the 'game' of using only positive words for a whole mealtime.

We enjoyed it, so we kept going. Over the next few weeks the older ones got stuck into some of the less complicated books, and even the younger two, then aged eight and six, had no difficulty at all in grasping the essentials.

Positive thinking helped us to feel calmer and more in control, and made us more able to help our bullied child recover some of his natural optimism and *joie de vivre*.

We went on to consider ways of creating an environment that would be particularly nurturing to self-esteem, and looked at how to meet the challenge of coping with unusually high levels of fear and anger in more robust and positive ways.

The programme we developed worked surprisingly well and all the ideas we used are brought together in this book. It's a brief and subjective selection, and if you want to explore any of the areas in greater depth I have included a further reading list at the end.

Some of the ideas may seem simple and obvious to you, and others difficult. You may not agree with all the suggestions; everyone's different. But I hope there will be something here that will help you to find a sense of direction and purpose, if what is happening has left you and your child feeling helpless and bewildered.

The book opens with a couple of chapters on how to establish the facts, find out what help is available and ask for help if you need it. The rest of the book is about how to develop good psychological self-defence techniques. I haven't made any distinction between different age groups of children, because this approach is about developing the robust attitudes in yourself that you want your child to have, and so providing a strong role model for him. Whether your child is five or fifteen, he will learn by what you are, so there's no need to tailor anything here to his particular stage of development.

I haven't distinguished either between the various sorts of people who might be doing the bullying. Although my child's experience was school-based, a lot of bullying occurs outside school and can involve adults as well as children. But whoever is doing the bullying, the effects on the person being bullied are the same, and this approach concentrates on tackling the effects.

By the same token, I haven't gone into all the different reasons why your child might be being bullied. Whatever their physical ability, ethnic origin, body shape or achievement levels, the effects are still the same.

The whole point about bullying for people who bully is to make someone else feel bad about themselves. Loss of self-confidence, low self-esteem, incapacitating anxiety and helpless rage are the effects the person who bullies is looking for. When he can no longer provoke them in your child he will find someone else to pick on.

There are several great advantages in this approach:

1. It feels safe and non-threatening
You are helping your child to develop the positive robust attitudes he needs in order to defend himself against bullying in less challenging areas of his life rather than in direct confrontation with bullies

2. It stops you making things worse

Concentrating on handling your own emotions more effectively means you can stay focused and positive and help to calm the situation down rather than increasing the tension by lashing out, getting into a panic or falling apart.

3. It protects your child from lasting harm

Bruises heal, but the psychological effects of bullying can cast a long shadow. Patterns of self-doubt and underachievement, unequal relationships, grief and anger can often carry over into adult life.

I heard a senior police officer speaking very movingly at an anti-bullying conference about the day his childhood experience of being bullied suddenly resurfaced during a family meal twenty years after he left school. Someone mentioned his child-hood nickname and he burst into uncontrollable tears, to his own and everyone else's great shock.

4. It means your child is less likely to become a victim in the future

Anyone can get picked on but bullies aren't famous for their courage and sense of fair play, so they're much more likely to choose a soft target, someone who can't defend themselves because they're crippled by self-doubt and self-dislike, than a person who isn't bothered by their nasty games.

5. Should the bullying continue, it will help your child to survive

Research shows that at least 5 per cent of children will be per-sistently bullied throughout their school life even in the most effective schools and realistically, for those children, it can just be a question of finding a way to get through without getting destroyed.

Often these are children who stand out in some way. They may be exceptionally attractive or clever or creative, for example, or they may not fit sexual stereotypes, or they may have special needs.

6. It will enable your child to ask for help if he needs it
A confident child who knows his rights and is willing to stick up for them is much more able to get help than one who is full of anxiety and self-doubt.

7. It will give your child invaluable skills for life
This is the unexpected icing on the cake, because the skills your child needs to handle bullying – feeling in control, holding on to his self-belief, being able to bounce back, facing his fears and channelling his anger – are the keystones for a successful life.

A staggering proportion of school children in every survey claim to have experienced bullying at school, many of them on multiple occasions. That means thousands of children are coping with being bullied and thousands of families are coping with a troubled child.

As far as I know, this is the only self-help book for parents that contains practical advice about how to cope with your own situation and at the same time help your child to cope with his.

CHAPTER ONE

Getting the Facts

The kind of facts you don't need to know, as a parent, are what proportion of boys or girls who bully have poor personal hygiene and what percentage of children under ten are 'very worried / a bit worried / not worried at all' about being bullied.

Focusing on statistics is unhelpful because it encourages you to think of children as 'victims' and 'bullies', instead of seeing the bullying situation as only a part of their lives. It can have you wondering what is wrong with your child that has made him into a victim or bully. This kind of approach is backward-looking and passive – it does nothing to make you feel less angry and bewildered.

If you want to move to the more active position of looking for solutions instead of explanations the only facts you need to know are:

- What is bullying?
- Is your child being bullied?

WHAT IS BULLYING?

Many children are themselves confused about what constitutes bullying. They may complain that they've been bullied because someone barged into them in the corridor, or their friend said something nasty to them during an argument. On the other hand, they may not realize they're being bullied when someone keeps teasing them really nastily, or even assaulting them, if they think of that person as a friend.

The two elements that define bullying are that it is persistent and deliberately hurtful. If someone repeatedly tries to hurt or upset another person in any way, you can safely assume that it's bullying.

There are two main categories of bullying – physical and non-physical.

Physical Bullying

This includes kicking, hitting, pushing, spitting, damage to property, theft and 'happy slapping'. The worst cases do seem to be becoming more violent, often involving weapons, but they only make the headlines because they are still thankfully very rare. Still, the fact that young people have been stabbed or raped at school makes the threat of physical bullying feel even more frightening for parents and children alike. Physical bullying is always wrong – there should be no grey area about that.

Non-physical Bullying

This includes teasing and name-calling, which account for up to 80 per cent of reported cases of bullying. Although the one being teased may experience this as extremely malicious, it can seem trifling to some children, who may genuinely think they're just having a laugh, and can be shocked when they find out how much distress they've caused.

But non-physical bullying also includes downright nastiness like making threats, spreading rumours, excluding from the group and a whole range of activities involving new technology such as:

- Abusive text messages and silent calls
- Bogus text messages sent in the name of the person who's being targeted
- Blue-jacking – anonymous messages sent to Bluetooth-enabled mobile phones
- Blog bullying – abusive comments included in a bully's weblog or abusive emails sent to victims' weblogs
- Bullying message boards

New technology has taken bullying out of the classroom and placed it into every area of victims' lives, so it can feel as if there's no escape. It also means people can be exposed and humiliated on a grand scale, not just in front of a few onlookers but in words and images that can be accessed by anyone, anywhere in the world.

Carly

When fourteen-year-old Carly stopped going out with her boyfriend, Jake, he began a campaign of abuse against her. He got all his friends to send text messages to her at the same time saying, 'We hate you. Just die.' He posted pictures on his school's intranet with her head superimposed on a pornographic image. He bombarded her blog with abusive emails, using different names so it looked as though lots of people were sending them. He also wrote insulting things about her on his own blog.

In a few short days, Carly's whole world fell apart. She couldn't go outside the house for fear of meeting someone who had seen the pictures or read the abuse, but she didn't feel safe indoors either because every time her mobile phone rang, it might be another abusive call. Also, she felt compelled to keep checking online to see if her ex-boyfriend had said anything even worse about her.

Carly became very anxious and depressed, and even thought about killing herself because it seemed the only way out.

In the past, people have tended to regard physical bullying as more serious than non-physical bullying, partly because the activities involved in physical bullying are illegal in adult life. But times are changing.

Psychological harm is now regarded as grounds for prosecution and there are laws against stalking and harassment. In one test case, a twelve-year-old girl had her claim of common assault against an older child upheld in court, even though the aggression she suffered was purely verbal. In another case, a boy who sued his school for failing to protect him from racist taunts was awarded significant damages. Non-physical bullying was also recently taken into account by the court when sentencing a boy who killed someone who had been bullying him for years – evidence taken in mitigation included humiliating photos posted on the internet which the bully had taken of him having got him drunk and stripped him naked.

We can only judge how serious bullying is by the intention of the bullies and the effects it has on the people involved, and this will depend on many factors other than what form the bullying takes.

One thing we can say categorically is that it is a very rare case of bullying which results in long-term physical damage, whereas all forms of bullying can leave psychological scars that last a lifetime.

For this reason, if your child seems upset and unsettled and you don't know why, it is certainly worthwhile trying to find out whether he's being bullied.

IS YOUR CHILD BEING BULLIED?

Quite often, parents have no idea their child is being bullied until a particularly nasty incident blows the whole situation wide open, or a teacher draws their attention to it, or the child suddenly breaks down. But more often than not there are small signs and symptoms of what is going on.

Some physical signs of bullying are:

- Cuts and bruises, lost dinner money, damage to clothes and property
- Minor ailments, like headaches and stomach upsets
- Eating disorders
- Sleeplessness and nightmares
- Bed-wetting

Some social signs are:

- Lack of enthusiasm about having friends over or going out
- Loss of interest in hobbies and pastimes
- Reluctance to go to school

Some psychological effects of bullying are:

- Heightened levels of anxiety and mood swings
- Outbursts of rage
- Destructiveness or self-destructive behaviour
- Bouts of apathy and depression
- Oversensitivity to criticism

There may also be a reduction of effort and competence in schoolwork.

The problem with the signs and symptoms of bullying is that they could all be signs and symptoms of something else. They don't prove that bullying is taking place – they indicate only that it's a possibility. They might prompt you to try making some discreet enquiries among trusted teachers or the parents of your child's friends. But the only way you can find out for certain whether your child is being bullied is by getting him to tell you about it himself.

Young children will often just come straight out with it. They are used to asking adults to sort out their problems for them, and they have more contact time with their teachers and parents, so there are lots of opportunities for talking. But older children are generally more reluctant to tell anyone they're being bullied. They tend to feel they ought to be able to sort it out on their own. They believe, often correctly, that their parents and teachers expect them to as well, and that therefore they'll be less willing to help. The bullying situation becomes a secret they're too ashamed to share.

Shame is one of the reasons why your child might not want to tell you he's being bullied, but there are lots more.

SOME REASONS WHY YOUR CHILD MIGHT NOT WANT TO TALK ABOUT IT

Fear of Reprisals

People who bully often use the threat of violence to stop their victims from telling anyone. Even when the bullying is purely verbal, children are usually afraid it might escalate.

In schools which have not succeeded in creating a strong anti-bullying culture there is also a very real risk that 'telling' will actually cause the bullying to spread, like in Angeline's story.

Angeline

Angeline and her best friend Roxy were the coolest girls in their primary school and they more or less had the power to decide who was in and who was not. But when they went up to secondary school, they got split up.

Without Roxy, Angeline felt vulnerable. The girls she'd had such power over in her old school started picking on her and shutting her out of the group, just as she had sometimes done to them.

After a miserable first term, Angeline told her form teacher what was going on. The teacher took the girls to one side and gave them a pep talk. But instead of making things better, this just meant they were nice to Angeline when the teacher was nearby and extra nasty as soon as his back was turned.

The girls told everyone that Angeline had 'dobbed them in', and soon all the children in the class were calling her 'teacher's pet'. But it didn't stop there. Her reputation spread, and even children she didn't know from other classes came up to her in the corridors and taunted her for being a dobber.

Ignorance

A lot of children don't understand that what is happening to them is bullying. Very young children may not even realize that kicking and hitting are wrong.

I remember when my first child started school. I was puzzled that, besides her four or five best friends, she wanted to invite one older boy to her birthday party. A week later I went to collect my child from someone else's party, and saw the same boy there as well.

'What's his secret?' I asked another parent as we waited for the last party game to finish. 'Why do all these little girls seem to have taken such a shine to him?'

The parent laughed out loud. 'They don't like him,' he told me. 'They're frightened of him. Whenever anyone's giving out invitations at school he jumps on them and threatens to give them a good kicking if they don't give him one too.'

My daughter confirmed this for me later, and I was really shocked. Why on earth hadn't she told me about it before?

'I just thought that was the way things were at big school,' she said.

Even much older children can fail to recognize they are being bullied, like Zack.

Zack

Thirteen-year-old Zack was part of a well-established group of friends. When he fell out with one of them, the whole group began to tease him. At first, it didn't bother him, but the teasing got worse until sometimes they were pushing him around as well, and then Zack started to get upset.

The boys told him not to be stupid – they were only having a bit of fun. Zack came to believe not only that he was a fat lump like they said, but also that he was the only one who had no sense of humour.

Resignation

Children often think they are being picked on because there is actually something wrong with them. If it's a thing they can change, like wearing unfashionable clothes or coming top in tests, they'll probably try to do something about it.

This is usually a waste of time and they soon come to realize that whatever they do, there's always something other children can tease them about. Then they join the ranks of people who are being taunted about something they obviously can't change, like the colour of their skin, and they can reach the conclusion that being picked on is just something they'll have to put up with for ever.

Denial

Many children who are persistently bullied can only cope by hoping against hope that if they just keep quiet and don't make too much fuss the whole thing will one day disappear all on its own.

Fears About How You Will React

The biggest fear most children have is that they won't be believed or taken seriously, and this does happen very often, in fact, as in the case of Danny and Juliet.

Danny and Juliet

Danny and Juliet had to play together sometimes because their mothers were friends. Juliet was slightly older than Danny. She was angry at being stuck with him, and often felt bored. She amused herself by ruthlessly taunting and intimidating him. When Danny eventually complained to his mother she said she was sure Juliet didn't mean anything by it, and she told him off for making a fuss.

Your child might also be afraid you'll react by:

- Taking the whole matter out of his hands, and deciding on a course of action without getting his agreement
- Criticizing him for getting into such a bad situation in the first place, or for not being able to sort it out for himself
- Offering him advice he can't take, like 'Tell your teacher' or 'Pretend you don't care', which will just make him feel worse
- Getting angry
- Getting upset

Before you decide to ask your child whether he is being bullied, take a few moments to think about the powerful reasons he might have for holding back. Feel the emotions. Then, if he refuses to talk about it or if he admits he is being bullied but won't go into detail, you'll be less tempted to badger him.

Trying to force him to open up about it will probably make him even more reluctant to do so.

> Have patience. Bullying is usually a situation rather than an event, and it's a situation your child has probably been in for a while if he's showing signs of distress. Do some research so you gain a real sense of the sort of thing your child might be dealing with, because the current situation is very different from when you were at school. I'd particularly recommend that you check out the websites at the end of this book.

Your child will cope for a couple more days while you update your ideas about bullying and set your mind on how to create the sort of conditions that will make your child feel it's safe to talk.

HELPING YOUR CHILD FEEL IT'S SAFE TO TALK

The first thing to think about is whether you actually have enough space for talking in your everyday life. Most of us don't have a lot of spare time and while some families are comfortable with setting aside a special time for conversation, over a family meal for instance, many others would find this artificial and embarrassing.

You don't have to drop everything and talk to each other all the time, but you do need to make it clear to your child that you are available if he wants to talk, and this means, of course, that you must actually be prepared to take a break if he wants you to and give him your full attention.

So, when your child comes into the room, stop what you are doing for a few seconds, look up at him and make a few opening remarks. He can then choose whether to stay and talk or go off and do something else.

If he stays, you will have an opportunity to work on the next thing you might like to consider – how do you talk to your child? Do you joke a lot? Do you tend to tease him? To disbelieve or belittle him? To patronize him? Do you talk about other people in disparaging ways? Simply noticing the sort of things you say can bring some big surprises.

I remember telling my family rather scornfully about a book I was reading in which one of the exercises was to go for a whole hour without criticizing anyone. 'How ridiculous!' I scoffed. 'Anyone could do that.' To my surprise and consternation, they challenged me to try. I lasted four and a half minutes. So now, not scornfully – not critically! – I recommend this exercise to you.

There are so many oblique ways of being critical. 'Seventy-six per cent? That's excellent! Just think what you could have got if you had revised more'; 'Your room's looking tidy – for a change'; 'I think I'd better do that for you'; 'What a nice colour – though I wouldn't have chosen it for myself'.

The key to avoiding being critical and judgemental is to focus on feelings. When you are talking, focus on your own feelings, and when your child is talking focus on his. For instance, instead of saying, 'My boss was being a pain in the neck today', you could say, 'I got really fed up with my boss today'.

If your child tells you that he didn't do as well as he'd expected in his science test you might be tempted to say, 'Never mind, it doesn't matter', but that would be your feeling, not his. You might say, 'That's awful! What went wrong?' but that would be your feeling too. Try saying you can see he feels disappointed; you know he was hoping to do well; you imagine it could really have spoiled his day.

> Listening with empathy is a skill that comes more easily to some people than to others. If you find it difficult, don't worry. Counsellors have to do special training to get the hang of it, and working at it on your own takes time. Just bear in mind that it's an option and use it when you remember to, which will often be when you've caught yourself saying something judgemental.

Focusing on your child's feelings will be particularly helpful when he finally plucks up the courage to talk about what's really troubling him because, when he offers you a clue, you won't miss it.

The clue could be something like this:

YOUR CHILD: I've got a sore leg.
YOU: Oh? How did that happen?
YOUR CHILD: Jamie tripped me up in football.
YOU: Was it an accident, do you think?

Your child shakes his head.

At this point, any of these responses will close the conversation down again: 'The little swine! I'll knock his block off when I see him!'; 'Where was your teacher, then? She really ought to deal with that kid'; 'Oh, dear! How could anybody be so horrible? I mean, I just don't understand it'.

If you want to encourage him to go on, empathize with him. This means validating his feelings and helping him to clarify them. It puts you on the same team.

YOU: I bet you felt pretty annoyed about that.

YOUR CHILD: I did. I got cross and then they all started laughing at me.

YOU: That must've been really embarrassing.

YOUR CHILD: Actually, they keep on doing it . . .

When he's ready, and not before, the whole truth will come out, and you can help your child enormously if you believe what he tells you, acknowledge his feelings and make sure you don't judge or belittle him.

WHEN THE TRUTH COMES OUT

As the details emerge you may well feel shocked, horrified, fearful and furious by turns or, of course, you may feel that he's making a big fuss about nothing. Either way, if you can stay focused on his emotions you're less likely to get carried away by your own.

You might be tempted to avoid the uncomfortable business of talking about such difficult things by taking action straight away or giving your child lots of advice and instructions, but this would not be in your child's best interests. What he needs in the first instance is not a champion or a teacher – he needs a witness.

Giving him a safe space to talk about what's happening to him will be helping him in three important ways. First, it will mean he no longer has to keep a secret, and secrets attract guilt and shame like jam attracts wasps. Second, it will enable him to release some of his pent-up emotions, and when strong emotions are bottled up they become even more dangerous because you never know when they might explode. Last, but not least, it will show him that you are committed to helping him to sort out the problem without disregarding his feelings and opinions or trying to take over.

Explain to your child that talking about problems is important as an end in itself, whether solutions emerge out of it or not. Tell him how beneficial it is to let his feelings out even if it's just to a pet or toy – they can certainly be relied upon not to overwhelm him with advice!

Suggest that if it's too hard for him to tell you all the details and he doesn't want to tell a friend or teacher, he might like to phone a helpline for a chat or have a few sessions with a counsellor. He might be happier to do this outside school if he feels sensitive about people knowing. You can find out about youth counselling in your area through Connexions, the national one-stop shop for everything to do with young people between the ages of thirteen and nineteen, or look under Youth Services on your local authority website.

Ask your child if he could try writing everything down. Sometimes that can actually be enough, as in the case of Dominic.

Dominic

Dominic's family were moving to a different area of the country and as he had always been a very sociable, confident child, he was looking forward to the adventure of starting a new school. But the transition didn't go smoothly and he couldn't seem to settle.

Within a few weeks, Dominic had become unhappy and withdrawn and his parents were really worried about him. As he couldn't tell them what was troubling him, they suggested that he write it down.

As soon as he started writing, Dominic found himself in tears. All the bottled-up emotions came spilling out. He had walked into the class so keen to make new friends but then, as soon as he opened his mouth, the other kids made fun of his accent. They mimicked everything he said, until he was afraid to say anything at all. Not talking made it impossible to make friends, and he felt isolated and rejected.

Reading back over what he had written, Dominic realized that it wasn't all the other kids who mocked him, but just one mouthy group. He felt angry with himself for letting them get to him but he knew it had only happened because they took him by surprise. Now he was ready for them and that meant he was able to start again.

> One of the least challenging ways your child can express himself is in a diary because it's private and no one is going to read it unless he asks them to. That means he can feel free to express all his most painful feelings without worrying about what other people might think. It will also provide an accurate record if he should decide later on to involve the authorities.

Finally, don't forget to praise your child for managing to talk about it, and to congratulate yourself on being able to be there for him. Your child can't begin to get to grips with his situation until he is able to talk about it, and you can't begin to help him until you know the facts. Opening a dialogue is the first and, sometimes, most difficult step. Keeping it open as things progress will also be very important.

For your child, talking is a way of freeing himself from shame, getting a more objective perspective and facing up to the fact that he has a problem. Having you listen is a way of feeling less alone.

When you both know exactly what is going on, you can sit down together and work out what you want to do about it.

RECAP POINTS

- Bullying can be physical or non-physical and frequently involves new technology
- Although physical bullying has become more violent in extreme cases, these are rare and most bullying is still teasing and name-calling
- The real long-term damage caused by all forms of bullying is psychological
- A bullied child may display a wide range of physical, social and psychological symptoms
- The first step in dealing with the problem is talking – this helps your child to release pent-up emotions and you to establish the facts
- You can help your child by staying calm, believing what he tells you and not taking control of the situation away from him

CHAPTER TWO

Approaching the School

If your child is being bullied by other children at her own school, the first thing you'll have to consider is whether to ask the school to take action. Interestingly, when you're thinking of telling the school what is going on you might find yourself holding back for all the same reasons that children hold back from telling their parents.

You might feel ashamed that your child has a problem, or if she's been picked on a lot you might think it's something she'll just have to learn to live with. You might want to ignore it and hope it'll go away on its own. You might be afraid the teachers will not believe you, or suggest you're overreacting, or take over and decide what to do without consulting you. You'll almost certainly feel worried that any action the school takes could make things worse for your child instead of better.

These are all perfectly reasonable fears. Parents who complain their children are being bullied are frequently perceived as being overprotective, especially if the bullying is non-physical. In such cases, intervention by the school sometimes does make matters worse.

So when you are considering whether to approach the school listen to what your child has to say about it. She's the expert. She knows how things are normally done, and her perceptions can tell you much more about the ethos of the school than any written policy document. What she has to say will not only help you to decide whether to go and discuss it with them, but also to know the kind of reception you might expect when you do.

However, if your child is extremely reluctant to inform the school, or if she has already done so to no avail, try not to let yourself be overcome by her fear and despondency. Even when effective action and advice is not forthcoming, opening a dialogue with the school can be helpful. It is empowering for you and your child to express your feelings about the situation and it disperses the unwholesome atmosphere of secrecy. It also means you are supporting the school in the fight against bullying because creating effective policies depends partly upon having a proper assessment of the general situation.

Reassure your child that she will be present at any meeting you arrange. Explain that you will not allow the school to take any action she does not agree with. But tell her that in certain circumstances it is almost always worth taking the risk and telling the school, especially when the bullying is physical.

PHYSICAL BULLYING – WHY IT'S A GOOD IDEA TO INFORM THE SCHOOL

Physical bullying always involves acts that outside school would be illegal. Schools have a legal duty of care for all their pupils, and they have to take every report of physical bullying seriously. You are not likely to be patronized or palmed off if you tell the school that your child is being physically bullied.

The illegal nature of physical bullying makes the question of punishment of offenders very straightforward, and most schools have effective disciplinary procedures that will come into play as soon as physical bullying is proven.

Incidents of physical bullying are easier to identify and prove than non-physical forms, and situations of physical bullying are easier to monitor. Some schools use closed-circuit television as well as adult supervision in the playground. Children who witness physical assaults can be in no doubt about what's going on, and some schools offer 'bully-boxes' and other discreet ways of informing on the perpetrators.

Furthermore, although I have heard some teachers take a 'boys will be boys' attitude towards playground violence, most people feel that physical assault is always unacceptable. Children who bully in physical ways put themselves automatically in the wrong, and their victims can usually be assured of sympathy and support.

Informing the school about physical bullying can feel risky, but it has a high success rate – in a major ChildLine survey, 80 per cent of children who reported physical bullying said their school took effective action. And the alternatives are generally worse. Just leaving it and hoping it will go away on its own is likely to result in an escalation of violence, with your child becoming progressively less capable of defending herself psychologically or physically. Expecting your child to tackle the people who are pushing her around is unrealistic because most bullying involves either a bigger child or a group of people picking on one weaker child, and some of them may even be carrying weapons. Besides, if your child did try to retaliate she might well find that she would be the one to get into trouble for bullying.

Taking the matter into your own hands by confronting the children who are bullying yours can be effective if they are still quite young, but it is more often than not a recipe for disaster. I have seen school problems develop into feuds involving whole families when parents have directly tried to resolve disputes. So go carefully on this one, and trust your intuition.

Moving school might give your child some respite, but you should be aware that sometimes the problem can follow the child and she may have to deal with the stress of moving and being the new class member as well as a fresh burst of bullying. If you decide to take this course, it might be a good idea to arrange some counselling sessions to help your child recover her self-confidence first, before she starts in a new location.

If the situation is very serious, or if your child has already tried several schools, you might consider taking her out of school altogether. This is a growing trend, and need not result in any loss of academic achievement, especially with modern online resources that offer advice, syllabuses and materials. Message boards and chatrooms mean that children and parents learning and teaching at home don't have to feel isolated but can see themselves as part of a home-schooling community.

However, removing children from mainstream education isn't a step that most parents have the time, the money or the confidence to take and, like changing schools, it has one major drawback – it avoids the issue rather than tackling it. Children who manage to stay put, to have faith in themselves and their teachers and to develop the inner resources they need to cope with the bullying situation can feel much better about themselves than those who feel they have had to run away.

So, if your child is being bullied physically, see if she will agree to you setting up a meeting with her class teacher, head of year or the senior teacher with responsibility for student welfare and discipline. Make sure your child is involved. Even if the school is already aware of the problem, discussing it in this three-way manner will show your child you support her 100 per cent, as well as letting the school know you are willing to do whatever you can to help.

STARTING A DIALOGUE

How you approach your first meeting with the school will determine how productive it is. If you allow your upset and angry feelings to take over, or adopt a confrontational attitude, you will probably succeed only in making your child more anxious and her teacher more defensive.

> The best way to contain your own feelings is by trying to empathize with those of the teacher. Bear in mind that she may also feel upset and angry about a child in her care being hurt and intimidated. She may feel responsible, or she may feel that she is being made responsible for problems that originate outside school, which families and communities are failing to address. She may be struggling to cope with a number of challenging and difficult individuals in a large class with little or no extra support. She will certainly be aware there's no easy solution.

In this meeting, try to stay focused on three main aims – to establish the facts, have your feelings acknowledged and agree a plan of action.

Establishing the Facts

It is helpful if you can provide accurate details about any bullying incidents you wish to discuss and this will be much easier if you or your child have kept a written record of events. You can download a record sheet from the ChildLine website or make your own.

A record sheet should include the date and time when each

incident occurred, where it happened, the names or descriptions of everyone involved, what was said or done and whether anyone else might have seen what happened.

If your child doesn't want to show it to anyone else, she can still use it to remind herself exactly what happened when it comes to talking to teachers.

It's up to your child how much she tells – if she doesn't want to name names, she shouldn't have to. Making the school aware that there is a problem in a general way is enough for them to be able to address it in a general way. It also alerts staff to the fact that your child may be at risk, so they can therefore become more vigilant.

Having Your Feelings Acknowledged

You have a right to be listened to and to have your concerns taken seriously. Don't be palmed off with platitudes. Be perfectly clear that whatever goes on outside school, inside school all social and behavioural matters are the school's responsibility. It is up to the school to take action, but if you are not happy about what sort of action is proposed your reservations should be respected.

Agreeing a Plan of Action

Most schools will have procedures for checking the facts when bullying is reported, and these might include interviewing everyone involved together or separately and getting written statements from the main players.

Once bullying is established, almost all schools will deal with it by punishing the ones doing the bullying and supporting the ones being bullied. Punishments can range from detentions to permanent exclusion. Support might include some form of counselling or providing a named member of staff that your child can go and see if she feels worried.

You might well feel it's perverse to offer counselling to your child instead of to the children whose uncontrolled aggression is what is causing all the problems, and in some enlightened schools the bullying child is perceived as the one who needs help and support. But your child might want to accept the offer, so don't be too quick to dismiss it on her behalf.

In fact, whatever your gut reaction to the measures the school suggests, try to bear in mind that they are dealing with problems like this all the time. They will probably have tried lots of different styles of punishment and support, and decided what works best for them.

Once you have agreed in principle what action should be taken, ask specifically what will be done to protect your child from any repercussions, and arrange a follow-up meeting to discuss how things are going.

WHAT HAPPENS NEXT?

This depends on the individual circumstances as well as the school's normal procedures, but any action the school takes should be quick and decisive.

Schools have been encouraged to adopt a conciliatory stance on bullying and use the 'no-blame approach' championed in

Britain by the government think-tank, the Anti-Bullying Alliance. This can sometimes be very effective, as in the case of Sherrie.

Sherrie

Twelve-year-old Sherrie was picked on by two older girls on the school bus. They teased her, went through her school bag and threw her things around, much to the amusement of the other children. After a few days of this treatment, Sherrie told her form teacher.

The form teacher took the older girls to one side and told them to stop or they'd be in big trouble. They didn't stop and the bullying got much worse, with the two girls manhandling Sherrie and threatening to beat her up if she told again.

Sherrie told her head of year, and she also mentioned that telling her form teacher had made things worse. The head of year talked to the older girls, saying he knew they weren't the kind of people who would pick on someone much younger and smaller than themselves – he imagined they just hadn't thought about the effect they might be having on Sherrie, and that probably they would like to apologize.

The older girls apologized to Sherrie, saying they had only been having a laugh and had never meant to upset her. Everyone knew it wasn't true, but treating the problem in this way made it possible for the bullying to stop without anyone losing face.

The no-blame approach can be very effective, especially with younger children where the problem comes from immature social skills, but it does have some drawbacks. For one thing, older and more vindictive children who really want to hurt their victim can actually derive satisfaction from hearing how much they are managing to upset her, and they may even gain information about her specific weaknesses. Trying to get them to empathize with her by showing how hurt she is will only humiliate her and increase their sense of power.

For another thing, if there's no blame there can be no punishment, and this means there's no redress for the victim and no deterrent for the bully. It also blurs the boundaries between right and wrong and so undermines the very social values we all want children to learn.

'No-blame' may not be enough on its own, but schools do also have a range of sanctions they can impose, from detentions to permanent exclusion.

When Adam was bullied, sanctions were used effectively against the ringleaders but the no-blame approach helped the rest of the class to understand and think about their own involvement.

Adam

Twelve-year-old Adam was picked on mercilessly by a group of boys in his class who called him names, kicked his chair, spat on his work and poked him with rulers in most of his lessons. Things got out of hand one day when the teacher was out of the room and Adam was punched and kicked in front of the whole class. His parents complained.

Their first meeting was with Adam's head of year. He immediately interviewed every child in Adam's class individually, and identified the two main culprits. He arranged meetings with them and their parents, and agreed punishments. One of the boys was excluded from school for a week and the other was put on report and ordered to attend three further meetings between his parents and the head of year to monitor his behaviour.

Adam was offered a place in a support group of 'vulnerable children', which he declined on the grounds that he didn't want to be singled out as odd or inadequate.

The head of year then talked to the whole class about the incident, encouraging them to feel empathy for Adam and to take responsibility for their part in what happened. Many of them subsequently apologized to him.

Adam's parents met the head of year a few days later, and were able to confirm that the physical bullying had stopped. They met him again after a month. The physical bullying had not resumed but Adam was being teased for telling, and they discussed ways to help him handle this.

It has been difficult in recent years for teachers to assert their authority because they only have a 'common law right' to mete out detentions and other punishments and that is no longer enough now that many parents are unwilling to back up the school. Some will even complain about their unruly children being disciplined. The government introduced new measures, unveiled in November 2005, that give teachers the statutory right to punish all forms of bad behaviour and to apply for parenting orders to force uncooperative parents to attend parenting classes.

IF NOTHING HAPPENS

If, after a day or two, nothing seems to have been done or if you are unhappy about your initial meeting, ask to see the head teacher. Again, try to adopt a non-confrontational attitude, establish the facts, have your feelings acknowledged and agree a plan of action.

If this meeting is unsatisfactory, or if there seems to be no follow-up, your next recourse is to the school governors or whatever authority administers the school. Many parents feel most comfortable talking to a parent-governor, but any member of the governing body will do.

After that, if you are still not satisfied, try making a written complaint to the head teacher, chair of governors or the governing body in question, giving all the facts and asking them to send you a plan of action in writing.

Who you contact next will depend on what type of school it is and where you live. In the UK, complaints should be addressed to the Director of Education for a local authority school, the diocese for a church school, and the Secretary of State for a grant-maintained school.

If all else fails, parents can take legal action, but fortunately it very rarely comes to this. Most schools do cope with incidents of physical bullying, even if it means shifting the problem outside school by expelling the children concerned.

Non-physical bullying, on the other hand, is different.

WHY NON-PHYSICAL BULLYING IS DIFFERENT

Physical aggression can be controlled in school, as it is in the community, by good policing and effective sanctions. But non-physical bullying is not about rules and laws – it's about values. Teasing, excluding, whispering campaigns and so on are not against the law unless they are so persistent and malicious as to amount to harassment or stalking, and people who engage in them can easily think they are not doing anything wrong. This makes the whole issue of punishment less cut and dried, and if the bully can't be punished it's easy for the victim to be seen as the problem.

In addition to this, many teachers still regard non-physical bullying as comparatively trivial, and can feel antagonistic towards people who don't share this view. Some teachers may even go so far as to publicly humiliate children who complain of being teased.

Polly

Polly asked her teacher if she could move to another table because the girls she sat next to kept whispering things about her and poking fun at her work. The teacher told Polly to stop being silly; all her classes sat in alphabetical order and she wasn't about to make an exception.

The girls found out what Polly had done and also how their teacher had responded, and that gave them open season to make her life a complete misery. Eventually, she snapped and ran out of the classroom when they were bombarding her with abusive notes across the table.

The next day, the teacher, who had got into trouble with the head for letting one of her pupils go running off in the middle of a lesson, said she needed someone to fetch her glasses from the staff room. 'You can go,' she told Polly, in front of the whole class. 'After all, you're such a good runner.'

All in all, if you decide to inform your child's school about non-physical bullying there is a chance that either no action will be taken or such action as is taken will actually make matters worse. Whether you decide to take the risk will depend upon your impression of the school, your assessment of the situation and how your child feels about it.

I think on the whole it is usually a good idea to open a dialogue, and you can always ask the teachers not to intervene directly. You will need to be particularly clear in your objectives and unwavering in your support for your child, because you are very likely to come up against attitudes like these:

'This school doesn't have a problem with bullying'

Subtext: 'You're the one with the problem'.

Bullying is a fact of life. 'This school doesn't have a problem with bullying' means 'This school doesn't care about bullying'.

'It's not exactly serious, is it – a bit of teasing and name-calling?'

Subtext: 'You're making a big fuss about nothing'.

Cuts and bruises heal, but sustained attacks on a person's self-esteem can have devastating effects. Studies show that non-physical bullying can leave emotional scars that are more painful and long-lasting than physical forms because it's harder to see what's going on and, as well as dealing with all the other strong emotions that kick in when someone is being bullied, victims can feel foolish or inadequate for getting upset about it.

In tribal communities, exclusion from the group is considered a more terrifying punishment than death. Non-physical bullying can drive children to despair. A few may resort to suicide, or suffer such a build-up of anger and hatred that they are driven to retaliate with uncharacteristic violence.

Most children rightly fear that verbal bullying can lead on to physical bullying if it is allowed to go unchecked.

'It's no good trying to protect children from the normal cut and thrust of life'

Subtext: 'You're an overprotective parent and your child is too sensitive'.

This is nonsense. Some teasing is normal in life, but very few people have to go to their place of work day after day knowing they'll be insulted and abused continuously, called names, spat on and universally despised. Very few people face being ostracized by their colleagues all the time.

Anyone who complains about such treatment is not being oversensitive – she's sticking up for her right to enjoy a normal degree of civility and respect.

'Boys will be boys' and 'Girls will be girls'

Subtext: 'Your child isn't a proper girl/boy if she/he can't accept behaviour natural to her/his gender'.

Sexual stereotypes are no more an excuse for bullying in childhood than in adult life. We don't say, 'Men will be men', and therefore brawl and beat their wives, and we don't say, 'Women will be women', and therefore spread vicious rumours and insult each other.

'This group may be high-spirited, but I wouldn't say they were bullies'

Subtext: 'Your child is lying'.

If at first you aren't believed, keep insisting until you are. The hardest part is telling someone for the first time – after that, it gets much easier.

'Your child is a bit of a loner'

Subtext: 'Your child is maladjusted and immature: she needs to change and be more sociable'.

Sociability is not a measure of maturity, it's a feature of personality. Trying to force a quiet child who is happy in her own company to become more sociable and outgoing is about as sensible as trying to make a clever child slow or a serious one laugh-a-minute funny. It devalues her gift of self-sufficiency and can make her feel there's something fundamentally wrong with her.

Unfortunately, you can meet this response even when the bullying is physical. In November 2005, the head teacher of a pupil who was stabbed in the head and chest at school is reported to have remarked that the bullied child had 'relationship problems'. This is extraordinary. Surely it's the ones who go around stabbing other people who have relationship problems?

All these attitudes condone bullying and put the bullied child at fault, and if you can counter them calmly and clearly your child will feel wonderfully supported and reassured.

You will gain insights into how much help the staff will be able to offer your child by simply noticing how you yourself feel after the meeting. If you feel blamed or criticized, ignored or belittled, that's how your child will feel when she tells. If you feel a sense of concern, co-operation and commitment, she will feel it too.

Of course, there are schools that take non-physical bullying very seriously and deal with it effectively, but I haven't mentioned them yet because it seems to me that if your child attends such a school she will probably be quite happy to sort things out with her teachers, and not involve you at all.

I heard a lovely story which perfectly illustrates this.

Emily
An eight-year-old girl went to her head teacher's office to complain that two other girls in her class had been teasing her and making her cry.

He brought the three girls together to talk about it. First, he asked the two who were teasing if they knew why he had asked them to come.

'It's because we've been teasing Emily, isn't it?' said one.

'That's right,' the head teacher agreed. 'And it's making Emily feel very unhappy. What do you think we could do about it?'

The two little girls looked at each other, and then they looked at Emily. Suddenly, one of them piped up, 'Well . . . we *could* stop teasing her.'

They both decided to write letters of apology to Emily, and the teasing stopped.

That wasn't quite the end of the story, though. When one of the parents saw her daughter writing her letter of apology she went straight to the school to complain that the head teacher had accused her child of bullying. It's just as well she took the child with her.

'But I *was* bullying!' the child protested, when she heard what her mother had to say.

If only things always went as smoothly as that!

The problem is that a really effective anti-bullying policy requires a lot of commitment from the whole school community, including the parents. It takes time and energy to create a strong ethos built on respect and civility, and it can also take money for training if some teachers are using sarcasm, ridicule and shouting to control their classes, for example, or some lunchtime supervisors favour turning a blind eye. Values can't be legislated for – they have to be learned by example.

Individual incidents of non-physical bullying can be dealt with most effectively in a school environment that wholly disapproves of all forms of bullying. Not allowing even the least serious offences to go unchallenged seems to cause a reduction in more serious offences too. But you have to be pragmatic. Teasing, excluding from the group and so on are very difficult to deal with because it's hard to tell whether they are driven by vindictiveness or immature socializing; there are no quick-fix solutions.

> If you don't feel confident that your child can be helped in direct ways by the school, see if there are any indirect ways they could help her. Providing somewhere safe for her to go at lunchtimes, reorganizing her classroom so that she never has to sit next to her tormentors or making sure that teachers arrive for lessons on time are all small things that could make a big difference.

NEW-TECHNOLOGY BULLYING

New-technology bullying takes the problem out of the classroom and into every area of a victim's life, which means reporting it to the school can rarely be the whole answer. But, unlike other forms of non-physical bullying, there is always evidence, so that at least means it will be clearer what is going on.

In a school situation new-technology bullying is invisible unless pupils report it, so it could be a good idea to talk to your child's teachers if only because then they will be on the alert and understand if your child seems stressed and unhappy. They can also tackle bullies about abusive text messages and warn them that if they don't stop they could be facing legal action.

A lot of children don't realize that cyber-bullying can count as harassment or stalking, and that because there is evidence it can be relatively easy to prove. They may not realize that almost any call, whether it comes from a landline or mobile phone, can be traced even if the caller withholds their number, or that all emails carry information about the path they've taken to get from one computer to another and therefore can be tracked.

When you're considering whether to involve the police, you need to take into account the duration and severity of the bullying. If you think it warrants legal action and your child agrees, get her to keep a record of the times and dates of abusive messages, to note what was said and any background noise she noticed, and to save abusive texts if possible. This will help the police and phone companies to work together towards a prosecution.

I would certainly recommend reporting any incidents of cyber-bullying that involve physical assault, such as so-called 'happy slapping' where mobile phones are used to record images of people being beaten up. These are sometimes sent to other mobile phones or posted on the internet, and they have provided proof in several recent prosecutions.

If your child is receiving abusive mobile phone messages and you don't want to involve the police you can still report the problem to the phone company and ask them to give your child a new number. You can also make sure your child knows how to handle abusive texts and phone calls, by never *ever* responding to them in *any* way. She only needs to keep evidence if she's planning to report the matter to the police or tell her teachers, so if the messages are relatively mild or infrequent or they don't bother her too much it would be best for her to delete them and keep her phone nice and unpolluted.

When it comes to abusive emails, tell your child never to respond to them or delete them but to forward them straight to the contact address for complaints of the sender's internet service provider. This will usually be something like abuse@hotmail.com or abuse@btinternet.com.

If your child is featured on an abusive message board, you can find an address to complain to in the 'help' section. Message boards set up by individuals are hosted by firms who will usually act quickly to shut them down, because allowing abusive material to be posted on them is against their terms and conditions.

> Cyber-bullying is particularly nasty and alarming but it is also easier to stop than more traditional activities like giving someone a kicking behind the bike sheds and frightening them into keeping quiet about it, or teasing and humiliating someone and pretending it's just a bit of fun.

We like to think the solution to bullying is simple – just tell an adult. But in the latest major ChildLine survey most children identified this as a risky strategy which can often make matters worse. I like ChildLine because they actually listen to what children have to say – and when your child is being bullied, so should you.

Take into account that there are benefits and risks for your child when it comes to telling. In the case of physical bullying the risks are lower, as the problem will be taken seriously, and the benefits are higher – your child probably won't be able to tackle it on her own. In the case of non-physical bullying the risks are higher and the benefits less assured. In the case of cyber-bullying, there are various people you could tell besides teachers without incurring any risk at all.

One more thing to put in the mix is this – telling the school if your child is being bullied means you will be contributing to a culture of openness about bullying in the school community as well as getting help for your child, and this will help the teachers create a strong anti-bullying ethos. Even if your child doesn't want you to talk about her particular problem you can still think about positive ways of getting involved. For example, you could research what strategies are used in your child's school and other schools so you can make useful suggestions; you could consider becoming a governor or talking to the PTA about ways of raising awareness of bullying through things like themed anti-bullying days. And you will certainly be thinking about other practical ways you can help to make your child's school a safer place for everyone.

In all your dealings with your child's school, try to stay positive and constructive. Back the school up whenever you can and try not to say anything that undermines the authority of the teachers. Always keep in mind that the teachers are on your side in the war against bullying.

Bullying is a complex problem that is deeply rooted in society and no school can work miracles. Your child has a legal right to physical protection, and she will have it, but it's much harder for schools to protect children from non-physical bullying and the unhappiness and loss of self-esteem that all forms of bullying can cause.

Fortunately, your child can learn to protect herself from being upset and undermined by bullying, and you are in an ideal position to help her.

RECAP POINTS

- Telling involves risk, so listen to your child's opinion
- If the bullying is physical it's usually a good idea to inform the school because they are likely to be able to deal with it effectively – and your child is not
- Non-physical bullying is different because it's hard to identify and prove, and therefore telling is less likely to lead to a solution, although it can still be worth opening a dialogue
- Cyber-bullying can take the situation out of school and you may need to talk to phone companies and ISPs rather than – or as well as – your child's teacher

CHAPTER THREE

Helping Your Child to Help Himself

The problem with most of the conventional advice to children who are being bullied is that it focuses on the child's behaviour instead of on his feelings. If he feels bad about himself and tries to act as if he doesn't, no one will be taken in by it, least of all himself. Besides, that would be concealing the problem rather than solving it. But if he feels good about himself, his behaviour will change automatically.

Emotions are the key to all forms of bullying. Making other people feel bad is the payoff for those who bully. For those who are bullied, the feelings of rage, anxiety and helplessness, as well as the consequent loss of confidence and self-esteem, are far more damaging than any physical effects, and will often last long after the actual bullying has stopped.

Many people think you can't change the way you feel, but you can. Your child can turn victim feelings of rage, anxiety and helplessness into detachment, confidence and power by changing the way he perceives the situation, developing a positive attitude, building up his self-esteem and learning constructive ways of dealing with anger and fear.

These are simple skills to master, as I shall be showing in the remaining chapters of this book, and you are in an ideal position to help your child because you will be experiencing exactly the same feelings in relation to the bullying situation as he is.

Just doing the work on your own will make a difference because it will help you to stay calm and feel more in control, and that will be reassuring for your child. It will also mean you can provide a better role model for him. But you might find it easier if you try out the ideas together with your child or your whole family, or at least talk about them with a friend or counsellor.

YOU ARE NOT ALONE

If you decide to get the whole family on board you don't necessarily have to tell everyone the reason why you're thinking of making the house a blame-free zone, creating a positive environment, and so on, because that might draw attention to your bullied child's problems in an unhelpful way. You might prefer to present the whole thing as an interesting experiment. Young children will be quite happy to treat it all like a game, and older children, who are becoming aware of different lifestyle choices, are usually curious to try anything new.

Explain what you are doing, and invite anyone who wants to join in. Make it clear that nobody has to if he doesn't want to. Congratulate yourself and each other when it goes right, and support yourself and each other when you find yourselves backsliding.

Even if some members of the family don't want to take an active part in the process they can help by listening to what you have to say about it and understanding what you are trying to do.

Your friends can help in the same way, by being sounding boards for the ideas you're working with. Naturally, they may not agree – I'm sure several of my friends and my children's friends probably thought we'd all gone a bit peculiar at times when we started to work in this way. But talking will help you get things clear in your own mind and besides, your friends might have some good ideas of their own to contribute about making positive change.

Who else can help? Well, you can sometimes gain strength by sharing ideas with people who understand what you are going through, and if you know of other parents whose children are having problems at school it might be a good idea to set up an informal support group. This could be a good forum for talking about self-help ideas, so long as it isn't allowed to degenerate into a place where everyone goes just to grumble and complain about the school.

You can also chat to other parents online. Two websites I

would strongly recommend are www.parentscentre.gov.uk and www.parentlineplus.org.uk, where you can discuss all your difficulties and dilemmas with other parents and put your questions to various experts in the field.

Talking always helps, and that goes for you as well as your child. There are various telephone helplines which offer a listening ear to parents as well as children, or you could book a couple of sessions with a counsellor. A lot of people have a strong resistance to the very idea of counselling because they believe it shows you're either crazy or inadequate if you need it. That's a pity because all it actually shows is that you're able to acknowledge a problem and are determined to sort it out.

Counsellors are trained to listen without being judgemental or interfering, and everything you say will be confidential. A counsellor could be particularly useful to you if you decide to work through the ideas in this book because he will be familiar with the concepts and used to working in this way.

> You should be a little cautious about choosing a counsellor because anyone can set themselves up in practice with very little in the way of qualifications and experience. Many health centres can provide counselling services, or at least advise you where you can get private counselling locally, or you could get in touch with the British Association for Counselling and Psychotherapy, who will have a list of accredited counsellors in your area.

Some counsellors with lots of experience are not BACP accredited simply because they trained before the scheme was introduced, so personal recommendation is another way of choosing who to approach. Fees are often negotiable, depending on your ability to pay.

All these people can help you if you want them to, so do bear that in mind as you and your child tackle the first great challenge of any self-help programme – letting go of blame.

LETTING GO OF BLAME

It's quite common for everyone involved in the bullying situation to blame somebody else. You might blame your own child or the child who is bullying him, his teachers or even society in general. Your child might blame the bullying child, his school, or you for not being able to sort it out. His teachers might blame all or any of the children involved and all or any of the parents.

The problem is that while everyone is sitting around blaming someone else, no one's actually doing anything about it. Blame makes you passive. Saying 'It's not my fault' is the same as saying 'I can't do anything about it', or perhaps even 'Why should I?'

If you want to take a more active and powerful position you have to let go of blame and accept responsibility. Like the no-blame approach, this is quite a sophisticated way of looking at things. It doesn't mean you should let go of the certain knowledge that bullying is wrong – people who vent their vindictiveness on those who are weaker, smaller or more vulnerable than themselves are always at fault. Nor does it mean shifting the blame to your child, whose 'weakness' might be that he is simply nicer, better socialized and less given to violence than the people who are bullying him.

We need to be able to blame other people for their wrongdoing in order to have certainty, to develop value systems and be able to stand up for what we believe in – in this case, you standing up for your child and him standing up for himself. But blame on its own is not enough. Letting go of blame means that even though you are completely clear in your own mind who is in the wrong, you move on from that to the 'and also' position of 'What can I do about it?'

RESPONSE-ABILITY IS POWER

However much everyone involved knows that the people bullying your child are in the wrong and should be stopped, there may be nothing you can do to force them to change their behaviour or to force the school to take effective action. This can leave you feeling helpless and frustrated.

But although you can't force other people to change the way they behave, you can change the way you respond and, interestingly, changing how you respond to other people is the most effective way of changing how they behave towards you.

For example, in the bullying situation, supposing your child is wearing a new coat to school for the first time. He's feeling pleased and proud because it's an expensive label and he thinks the other kids will all be jealous of him. He gets a few admiring glances as he walks into school but then one of the other boys says loudly, 'Nice coat – shame about the colour!' and everyone turns to look.

Your child could respond by feeling crushed and humiliated. He could think, 'Why did I choose this colour?' or even, 'How could Mum and Dad have let me be so stupid?' He could feel that the new coat is spoiled now and there's nothing he can do about it and it's the other boy's fault for being horrible.

If he responds like that then after school, he'll stuff the coat in his bag and pretend to be warm enough even if it's blowing a gale. What will the other children think, especially the boy who was mean, when they see your child shivering in the bus queue? Is he more likely or less likely to tease your child again?

But now supposing your child chooses a different way of responding, refusing to let the other child spoil things for him. He could think, 'Actually, I like this colour, so stuff that!' Then his body language will say he still feels pleased and proud and that will mean the other kids go on giving him admiring glances – and where will that leave the bigmouth? Who's the loser now?

You can test out for yourself how changing your responses to other people changes the way they behave towards you. Supposing you always pass the same person on the way to work and he always ignores you so therefore you ignore him. Try saying a cheerful 'Good morning'. Keep it up for a couple of days and before long he'll be saying a cheery 'Good morning' too. A simple thing like this can change the way you perceive people and are perceived by them, as well as radically altering the way you relate to each other.

Try it within the family. Maybe your partner gets stressed and shouts a lot, and you always end up shouting back. You wish they wouldn't do it and you blame them for all the rows. Well, maybe you can't stop them shouting but you can choose how you respond to it, so don't give away your power by getting drawn in. Stop shouting – simply refuse to raise your voice. Keep it up for a couple of days and notice what effect that has on how much your partner still shouts at you.

If you normally end up shouting at your children try the same thing with them. Make up your mind that you will not raise your voice, and see what effect your unilateral action has upon the general level of noise in the house. It might surprise you.

Getting people to change how they behave towards you by changing how you respond can work in more mysterious ways as well. Does someone you know have a habit that really annoys you? If you stop reacting with annoyance two really interesting things happen. First, it stops bothering you and next, it stops.

If your child can stop caring about the teasing and name-calling, the teasing and name-calling will stop. But the only way he can begin to stop caring is by taking responsibility for his own emotions. This means shifting the focus from 'them' ('They're making me feel bad', 'They're upsetting me') to 'me' ('I'm letting them make me feel bad' and 'I'm letting them upset me').

You can't make him take responsibility by telling him to, but in this as in all other areas, you can get the change you want in him by making changes in yourself. If you can change the way you respond to setbacks in everyday life and explain what you are doing, you will set an example of blame-free attitudes that will soon rub off on him.

CREATING A BLAME-FREE ZONE

Blamefulness is part of the victim adjustment and it will be harder to trigger in a child whose family doesn't use the blame game. The most effective way you can help your child not to get stuck in blame is by making your household a blame-free zone. A simple way to start is by banning the b-word and the f-word.

The B-Word and the F-Word

In our family life, the b-word is 'blame' and the f-word is 'fault', and they are as unacceptable as the other b- and f-words.

If you ban these words you will instantly become aware of all the ways we imply blame without naming it and that will help you to notice and root out any implications of blame.

For example, imagine you're washing up and your child is grumbling about having to dry. You break a plate. Your first impulse might be to say, 'That was your fault for making me feel stressed out!' If you had to avoid the f-word you might say instead, 'Look what you've made me do!' or 'I wouldn't have done that if you hadn't been giving me so much earache!' But if you let go of even the implication of blame then you have no choice but to take responsibility – the fact is it was you who broke the plate.

Not blaming other people has the added bonus that it makes it much easier for them to take responsibility themselves. If you break a plate and say, 'That was your fault,' you automatically put your child on the defensive and he's bound to react by saying, or at least thinking, 'No it wasn't!' But if you refrain from blame – 'Oh, dear, look what I've done' – it's much easier for him to notice and acknowledge his part in the problem: 'Sorry, Mum. I shouldn't have been making such a fuss.'

The words 'fault' and 'blame' are the tip of the iceberg which draws your attention to what's underneath. Here are some other subtle ways you might notice yourself shifting responsibility on to your child:

- 'You're making me worried/angry/unhappy'
  It's up to you how you feel so just say, 'I feel worried/angry/unhappy'.
- 'You mustn't upset your father/mother/grandmother'
  It's up to father/mother/grandmother how they feel so don't be tempted to use them as a lever. There's no need to bring them into it at all.
- 'I can't cope if you don't behave'

Your ability to cope should not depend on your child making things easy for you. Accept his behaviour like any other challenge life presents you with. You wouldn't say, 'I can't cope if I get flu / have an accident / burn the pizza', because there would be no point. No one else can protect you from these difficulties. Don't ask your child to protect you from the normal challenges of being a parent. If you really can't cope then it's up to you to get some help.

- 'You're being difficult'
  If you find your child difficult, that's your problem, not his. So say, 'I'm finding your behaviour difficult' instead.

As you begin to take conscious responsibility for your own actions and feelings, your child will see how to take responsibility for his. Being responsible is far less comfortable than blaming someone else and you will make it easier for him if you resist the temptation to try to protect him.

You might think, for instance, that you're being understanding and sympathetic by taking the attitude that he's bound to feel upset by the bullying situation, that he's perfectly normal and it's not his problem. He is normal, but if he's upset by bullying then he does have a problem and he needs to find more than his normal resources to solve it. Trying to comfort your child in this way will only make his response to the situation feel inevitable and discourage him from feeling empowered to change it.

It may seem harsh to tell your child that he's letting the children who are picking on him make him feel angry and frightened, but actually it's a way of helping him to take control.

As you start to notice all the ways you shift blame on to other people you will also notice all the ways they try to shift blame on to you. After all, if it's up to you how you choose to respond to other people then it's up to them how they choose to respond to you. As soon as you stop thinking that it's someone else's fault when you feel irritable or upset, you'll also stop thinking that it's your fault when they do. The glorious upside to letting go of blame is that you also find yourself breaking free from guilt.

Bullies love to play the blame game. They say things like 'You made me do that' and 'You brought it on yourself'. They say 'You're overreacting' and 'I only said those things because they're true'. It's a double-whammy because it makes the target feel bad both for being picked on and for causing it to happen. As your child learns to take control of his own emotional reactions to things he'll see more clearly that other people can take control of theirs.

Sam

Sam was having trouble with Aaron, another boy in his class, who kept making fun of him for being fat. If Sam was slow to understand something in class, Aaron said it was because his brain was made of lard, and between lessons Aaron would push him roughly aside, saying he was clogging up the corridor.

When Sam complained about it, Aaron said, 'You shouldn't be so fat and stupid – you really get on my nerves.'

For a while, Sam believed it really was his fault that Aaron was being horrible to him, but then his friends said, 'Why are you letting him get to you?' Sam saw that just because Aaron said vile things to him he didn't have to believe them – and then he realized that just because Aaron didn't like fat people he didn't have to be nasty to them. It was up to Aaron to sort out his aggression just as it was up to Sam not to let it make him feel bad about himself.

It takes persistence and determination, but most of all it takes clear thinking, if you want to stop blaming other people for your bad feelings and not let them blame you. Picturing bad feelings as something concrete that gets passed around from one person to another can help you to be more aware of what's going on.

When anyone tries to dump their bad feelings on me I find it helpful to visualize their anger, resentment, jealousy or whatever it is as a hot potato. I'm sorry they're finding it too hot to handle, but I don't hesitate to give it back.

THE GAME OF HOT POTATOES

Your child can think of bullying as a game of hot potatoes. He can see the bully as a person with bad feelings he can't handle. He only needs to notice his own feelings to realize that you don't even think of hurting other people when you feel happy – it's only when you're in a bad mood that you need someone to take it out on.

It may be hard to understand why your child's tormentor is feeling bad because children who bully don't fit any stereotype of deprivation and abuse. Children from successful, wealthy backgrounds can have less obvious pressures to bear, like the weight of unrealistic parental ambitions, for example, or negative undercurrents in their family relationships.

Often, there are clues in the nature of the bullying. A girl who feels anxious about her body shape might tease someone else for being fat. If she can make her victim start to worry about her body shape then the bad feeling is precisely transferred.

A boy who wants to work hard and achieve well but is afraid of being teased for his keenness might tease someone else for being too keen. If he can make his victim feel worried about working hard and doing well then the bad feeling is precisely transferred.

Even quite young children can easily grasp this concept. I was talking to an eight-year-old who had been teased all summer for having fat legs, and this had made her too embarrassed to wear shorts and skirts. When I explained to her about the hot potatoes she thought for a few moments and then remarked that she had, in fact, noticed that the girl who teased her always wore long trousers herself.

From then on, this child wore shorts. When I saw her again, I asked if she was still being teased.

'Oh, no,' she told me. 'I talked to that girl on her own, and told her I was sorry she felt she had fat legs, but personally I thought they were just fine!'

Sometimes, the hot potato gets passed around with the bullied child taking out his anger and anxiety on someone else so that he becomes a bully too. Very often a child who doesn't dare to express his rage and frustration at school will let it all out in the comparative safety of his home. If your child does this to you he will be giving you the perfect opportunity to show him how to refuse to be bullied by giving the hot potato back.

Imagine your child has been teased at school about wearing glasses. As soon as he gets home he starts shouting at you for not letting him have contact lenses and demanding that you take him straight to the optician's to order some.

You would be fully justified in feeling angry, hurt and bewildered by this unprovoked attack, especially as he knows you can't afford to pay for contact lenses, but that would be giving your child a model of victim attitudes and doubling the level of anger and anxiety in the situation.

It would be much better to acknowledge your child's bad feelings, but make it perfectly clear those feelings belong to him. Not allowing him to make you angry and upset means you will be able to feel sympathetic towards him rather than resentful. What's more, he will feel safer because his bad feelings are contained, and he won't have to carry any extra burden of guilt.

So just tell him you can see he's upset and it must be hard having to wear glasses all the time, but just at the moment you really can't afford them and besides, the optician did recommend waiting until he's at least sixteen.

A simple technique for giving the hot potato back is called 'fogging'. This is a useful skill for anyone who often has to cope with other people's aggression. It means putting up a smoke-screen to conceal your own views and values by appearing to agree with your aggressor. 'You could be right', 'Thank you for pointing that out', 'I'll certainly give this some thought' and so on are great ways of defusing aggression. Keeping your own opinion hidden means you don't take anything personally, or feel the need to retaliate.

Giving the hot potato back is not about retaliation. It's about refusing to be involved in someone else's problem. Being clear that people who bully have a problem makes it easier to let go of blame.

Although the problem is often to do with bad feelings, it can sometimes come from a lack of good feelings like kindness and concern. A child who seems popular and well adjusted, and has no particular urge to hurt anyone, can behave in hurtful ways simply because he lacks empathy. Small children are very self-centred, and they have to learn how to be sociable by becoming aware of other people's feelings. Children who bully because they lack empathy have failed to mature in this way. They can find it difficult to make healthy relationships in later life.

Other children who don't have problems with aggression or lack of empathy may become involved in bullying because they lack self-confidence. These children are so desperate to belong or so afraid of becoming victims themselves that they are willing to put their own moral scruples to one side in order to co-operate with a bullying gang. They will be particularly vulnerable to peer pressure in other areas such as drinking, smoking and drugs.

Seeing people who bully as having a problem can help us to be less blameful. Here are some more ways of avoiding blame.

MORE WAYS OF AVOIDING BLAME

Focus Forwards

Blame is always in the past so one very easy way of not getting stuck in it is focusing on the future. Supposing you're cross because your partner forgot to pick up a pizza for the children's tea . . . you could steam about it all evening and make everyone suffer, including yourself, or you could just get on and think about what you're going to do about it now. Maybe your partner could pop back out to the pizza shop, or the children could have beans on toast for tea.

Use 'When you . . . I feel . . . because'

This is a great little formula to remember if you want to avoid saying things like 'You make me feel so angry!' For example, if your child never tidies up after himself, so that it feels as if you're forever collecting up his dirty dishes and putting his crisp packets in the bin, you might get really cross and say, 'Sort this mess out right now! How can you be so untidy? You treat this place like a hotel,' and so on.

If you use the formula you can *say* you feel cross instead of acting it out, and it means you can take responsibility for your own feelings. 'When you leave lots of mess lying around I feel angry because it's a lot of work keeping the house tidy and it would only take you a few seconds to tidy up after yourself.'

Don't Label

Labelling children as 'victims' and 'bullies' means identifying the problem as something wrong with them rather than their behaviour. It ignores the other aspects of their personality – the caring side, the powerful side – that will enable them to alter their behaviour, and so it removes the feeling that they are capable of change.

It can be helpful to avoid labelling people generally. 'You're a naughty boy' is more crushing and negative than 'That was a naughty thing to do', for example. 'Your teacher is hopeless' is more judgemental than 'Your teacher doesn't seem to have handled that incident well'.

Accept that Nobody Behaves Perfectly

We all indulge in bullying behaviour from time to time. Everyone sometimes takes out their bad mood on someone else, whether it's by yelling at them or giving them the silent treatment. Everyone says tactless and hurtful things, and everyone will occasionally be willing to exclude people they don't feel like socializing with. Not being blameful when other people do it means not having to beat yourself up about it too much when you do it yourself.

Don't Judge

> Demonizing the child who is bullying yours is not a good idea. People on both sides of the bullying relationship can feel better about themselves by denigrating the other. Just as the one who bullies can feel stronger, braver and more in control because he sees his victim as weak, cowardly and at his mercy, so the one who is bullied can feel that he holds the moral high ground if he sees the bully as wicked and wrong. He may risk becoming one of those people who prefer to be right than happy.

Ask Yourself, 'How else might this situation serve my child?'

Being a victim could have other payoffs besides making your child feel good and innocent in contrast to the bad, guilty person who is bullying him.

If he has poor self-esteem, for example, it can reinforce his low opinion of himself. This might not seem like much of a payoff, but the fact is that however sad or self-limiting their world-view, people feel reassured by things that support it and threatened by things that contradict it. So if your child's experience of himself is as someone who doesn't deserve to be liked, being bullied could feel entirely appropriate to him. If he's very self-critical, other critical voices will simply validate his own.

Other payoffs to consider are that if your child is stressed by any aspect of school life, bullying might give him a welcome excuse for going to ground, and if he has worries or difficulties outside school it might create a distraction.

It's hard to accept that such a horrible situation could have some payoff for your child, but it's worth considering if you can. Look at the effects of the bullying on your child and your family. Is it making him a focus of attention? Is it distracting you from the new baby / your job / the house / work or relationship issues?

Your bullied child did not consciously ask to be bullied, but if it has payoffs for him that you don't address it will be harder for him to break out of it.

Letting go of blame means not waiting for someone else to change, but being ready to sort things out for yourself. It's a wonderfully empowering thing to do. But how can your child go on to sort out such an alarming problem as bullying? How can he start to feel good about himself again? How can he ever stop feeling frightened and intimidated, or cope with such an intensity of rage?

The answer is that he can't do it all straight away. He's like a mile-a-day jogger who has decided to run a marathon – he will need to build up his general fitness first.

The fitness your child needs to combat his self-doubt, fear and anger is not physical. He needs to build up his inner resourcefulness, and you can help him to start by creating a blame-free atmosphere at home.

RECAP POINTS

- Letting go of blame is the first step because it frees your child to focus on what he can do to help himself
- This does not mean you should be any less clear that the children bullying your child are in the wrong
- It represents a pragmatic acceptance that you may not be able to stop people being nasty but you can stop letting them make you feel miserable
- You can help your child to experience the empowering effect of taking response-ability by modelling it and making your home a blame-free zone

CHAPTER FOUR

Nurturing Positive Attitudes

Even the most robust and optimistic child can have her confidence in herself and her world worn down by persistent bullying. Even the most successful parents can begin to fall prey to self-doubt, and question their past behaviour and future ability to cope. The whole family can find itself on a downward spiral of negative and catastrophic thinking that flushes away all its energy and resourcefulness like water disappearing down a plughole.

Positive thinking is the plug!

POSITIVE THINKING

The idea of positive thinking is that your experience of life depends not on what happens to you but on how you interpret it. So life is not something you suffer – it's something you create.

Positive thinking is an attitude of mind that is active rather than passive, and that makes it a step in the right direction for anyone stuck in the bullying situation.

If you haven't come across positive thinking before, you will probably have your doubts about it at first. It does seem to involve a lot of denial, and you may feel that it requires you to turn your back on the harsh realities of life. But it's easy and interesting, so why not give it a go? My children wanted to join in too, but if yours don't, it doesn't really matter. Positive thinking is infectious – if one person gets it then those around them will soon catch on.

The easiest way to get the hang of positive thinking is to start with positive words.

Positive Words

The positive approach to language turns conventional thinking on its head – it sees language not as describing experience but as creating it. It reverses the normal sequence of 'Be – Think – Say' and proposes a new sequence of 'Say – Think – Be'.

For example, supposing a man says he has a good job. We might assume he says it because he thinks it, and he thinks it because it is indeed a good job. That's 'Be – Think – Say'. But the positive approach to language suggests the process can work in reverse; if a man says he has a good job often enough he will come to believe it, and then it is indeed a good job for him. Say – Think – Be.

It follows from this that you can choose to have positive experiences by choosing to use positive language. If you avoid using expressions like 'I can't' or 'It's impossible', you stop putting restrictions on yourself. In arguments, changing 'Yes, but' to 'Yes, and also' stops you putting restrictions on others.

Thinking about the words you use in the family situation can make a surprising difference. Thinking about the words you use in your own inner dialogue can be very fruitful too. Take the bullying situation. The 'Be – Think – Say' pattern might go something like this.

Your experience has been of a bad situation which has not got better, and which no one has been able to resolve. That's the fact. It leads you to think that the problem won't get better, and no one will be able to resolve it. Then your self-talk may be along these lines – 'She's never going to cope', 'I can't help her', 'The school should do something about it'.

The positive approach is to change your self-talk. Then the way you perceive the situation will be affected, and that will affect the situation itself. What if, when you think about the bullying problem, you notice your negative self-talk and opt for positive alternatives? 'She is coping', 'I am helping her', 'The school is doing something about it'.

The more you repeat messages of this kind the more you will notice the truth in them. There will be ways in which your child is coping, and ways in which you are helping, and it is possible that the school is doing something about it.

Such a pattern of thinking is less alarming and more hopeful. It will enable you to stop adding your own burden of helplessness and anxiety to your child's, and that will make her situation less overwhelming. She will cope better, you will be helping. Say – Think – Be.

Affirmations

Positive self-talk can take the form of affirmations, which are a sort of benign brainwashing and they work like this. You decide what you want, and affirm that you've already got it. You use the present tense, and support it with expressions like 'right now' and 'at this moment' because in the present moment, released from the negative past and anxieties about the future, everything is possible.

Your conscious mind might balk at the obvious discrepancy between what you are saying and what the actual situation is, so it can feel strange and silly at first. But so long as you keep repeating your affirmation whenever you think of it throughout the day your unconscious mind will simply accept the message in the words.

So if, for example, you feel you are a hopeless parent for not being able to help your child, you don't say, 'I wish I were a great parent' or 'I hope I can become a better parent'. You simply affirm:

RIGHT NOW, I AM A WONDERFUL,
SUPPORTIVE PARENT!

You keep on saying it until you start to believe it. Then your anxiety and inhibitions begin to dissolve, and you are able to release the wonderful parent in yourself. For, whatever the enterprise, fear of failure and lack of confidence are bound to compromise your performance and prevent you reaching your potential.

When you use affirmations, avoid negative words altogether.

'It's a great day today', for example, has a much more punchy feel than 'Today is not too bad'.

I have seen claims that even affirmations like 'I am now fabulously wealthy' can come true, and I suppose they can, in the sense that they become possible. You have to be able to conceive of something before you can hope to achieve it.

Some people are quite comfortable affirming things they don't consciously believe in and allowing them to work their magic, but others prefer to choose affirmations that feel more realistic. It probably just depends how good you are at suspending disbelief. If 'Right now, I am absolutely gorgeous' feels like a bit of a stretch, try 'Right now, I am looking good' or 'Right now, I am happy with the way I look'.

Try an affirmation now before you read on. Think of something negative that you often say to yourself, such as 'I'm so stupid' or 'I'm just unlucky'. Repeat it a number of times, checking out the emotions that arise and the way your body feels the longer you keep it up.

Stop and turn your negative self-talk into a positive affirmation – 'Right now, I am a wise and intelligent person'. 'Right now I am a lucky person'. Say it a few times. Be aware of what's happening in your emotions and your body as you go on repeating it.

Write your affirmation down on a piece of paper and put it somewhere you'll see it lots of times throughout the day – on your desk, say, or the kitchen counter. Put it on Post-it notes and stick them on your mirror, your fridge and your computer, and every time you see one of these reminders repeat the affirmation several times and notice how you feel. If that's too embarrassing because everyone else will read it, just memorize it and use a secret reminder – put on a garment or piece of jewellery you don't usually wear, for example, or carry a token of some kind in your pocket or handbag.

You can have a lot of fun with affirmations. You can also use them to get you through your darkest hours. Your children might be able to use them too. Share them, talk about them. Even your bullied child might find she can believe 'At this moment, I am strong and beautiful and brave!'

Positive thinking shows that by choosing positive words you can create positive experience for yourself, and that is an incredibly exciting thought. Cognitive behavioural therapy – CBT – uses the same idea but develops it. Instead of drowning out negative thoughts by repeating positive ones, CBT engages with the negative thought, examines it, challenges it, and uses common sense as a pathway to the positive.

Which one works best for you will depend on what kind of person you are. If you find the suspension of disbelief comes easily to you, positive thinking could be a very effective way to work but if you favour logic over imagination, you might be more comfortable with the cognitive approach.

THE COGNITIVE BEHAVIOURAL APPROACH

Cognitive behavioural therapy is very effective at dealing with stress, anxiety and depression, and as it's a bit more scientific than positive thinking a lot of people feel more comfortable with it.

The basic idea is the same – that we create our own experience.

It isn't the events that happen to us that determine whether we have a happy or unhappy life – what matters is how we interpret them. As Shakespeare said, 'There is nothing ever good or bad but thinking makes it so'.

According to CBT, how you think about what happens will affect how you feel about it and that in turn will affect your behaviour. For example, supposing there's a rail strike and you can't get to work. You could think, 'This is a disaster! I'm going to have such a backlog tomorrow. I'll never cope!' If you think like that you'll feel stressed and unhappy all day. If you feel stressed and unhappy, you won't be able to settle to anything, and maybe you won't sleep too well either through worry.

The likely outcome of this scenario is that by the time you do get back to work you'll be feeling tired and anxious and you really won't be able to cope very well with the backlog. As if that isn't bad enough, your negative experience of this rail strike will mean you'll feel worried in case it happens again, and if it does you'll take what happened this time as proof that it's going to be just as bad again. And so the cycle continues.

But supposing you responded to the rail strike in a more positive way? You might just as well choose to see it as a great opportunity to have a day out doing something you really want to do or simply recharging your batteries. If you think this way, you'll feel happy and relaxed. Feeling happy means you'll have an enjoyable and fruitful day, and probably sleep like a baby. That means you'll go back to work feeling refreshed and ready to tackle the backlog, and you'll whiz through it. What's more, you won't be at all worried about the possibility of another rail strike because you've just had proof that it could actually be a bit of a bonus.

The key thing about CBT, as about positive thinking, is that you have a choice about how you perceive things. This can come as a complete revelation because the way you respond to experience is normally automatic and you don't even notice what you're thinking let alone the effects your thoughts have on your moods and behaviour.

Family Lore

Where do our automatic responses come from? Well, most of them are formed within our families of origin – for example, if your parents were always bracing themselves for disaster then you might have grown up assuming a pessimistic outlook, but if they took the view that everything always turned out all right in the end then you'll probably have developed that assumption yourself.

You can spot family attitudes in the mottoes and catch phrases that underpin your family lore. 'No good will come of it', 'I don't know why I bother', 'Don't get your hopes up', 'Life isn't fair', 'I want never gets', 'Onwards and upwards', 'Do as you would be done by', 'It'll all come out in the wash'. Do any spring to mind when you think about your childhood home? If not, keep it in mind – you'll soon notice them when you say them to your own children.

Family mottoes are often unconsciously echoed in songs. What songs do you remember your parents humming or singing to themselves? What did they like to listen to? When you find yourself humming or singing little snippets of songs, notice the words. Is there a reason why they could have popped into your head right now? What songs do you frequently find yourself humming?

The sort of family motto I grew up with was 'Don't let them grind you down' and 'Mustn't grumble!' – attitudes which were strongly shaken by the bullying situation. And that's the thing about automatic attitudes – they aren't written in stone. The ways of thinking that you absorb from your family can be challenged and changed by your life experience.

Sometimes a single experience can change the way you think about the world – a death in the family, for instance, can make some people find faith and others lose it – and then that's a pivotal point. Whatever religious assumptions you grew up with can be outgrown and replaced by other ones, and then your automatic response to adversity will be different.

A single experience can change your assumptions about yourself as well. Supposing your teacher once told you that you were tone deaf – even if you come from a family of lusty singers who think that everyone can sing, you might still end up convinced that you couldn't, and then that would become your new automatic thought whenever the band struck up. Supposing you were mocked at school about your weight – your family attitude might be that size doesn't matter but you could still come to believe that it's important, that you're too fat, and that being fat makes you an ugly person. Now your automatic thought is 'Fat is ugly' and 'I am fat'.

Often, children who are bullied come from families where the assumption is that people normally behave in a civil way towards each other and problems can be sorted out by sitting down and talking about things. Cruel, hurtful, aggressive behaviour can feel very confusing to a child who thinks like that, and the only logical conclusion may be that something really is wrong with her to make other children be so abnormally vindictive. It may be necessary for you to let go of your idealistic assumptions and acknowledge that sometimes people are horrible to each other just because they can be, and there's a whole side to human nature that actually isn't very nice.

Societal Influences

Besides your family of origin and formative life experiences, you can absorb the assumptions of the society you live in like a sponge on a wet surface. Daniel Goleman, in his book *Emotional Intelligence* (Bloomsbury, 1996), talks about a 'modern epidemic of depression among young people'. He ascribes this to pessimistic habits of thought that make children respond to relatively minor problems, like an argument with their parents or a bad grade, by becoming depressed. Negative thoughts that become part of an 'epidemic of depression' have to be part of the whole culture.

Your child is growing up in a time when the media dominates everyday life. What assumptions might she make from watching television? From watching the news, the assumption that the world is full of evil and violence and that it's necessary to point the finger of blame. From soaps, that friends betray each other and families fall apart. From makeover shows, that we aren't good enough just the way we are. From commercials, that we need lots of things we haven't got in order to be happy. And from game shows and comedies, increasingly, that it's funny to mock, abuse and belittle people.

When you add to this the assumptions of the education system your child is working within – that everyone should succeed within a narrow range of academic tasks, using a narrow range of methods no matter what their natural aptitudes and learning styles – then you can see that her thinking might well be making her more vulnerable to bullying. A little cognitive spring-clean could be helpful.

As with all the ideas in this book, try the cognitive behavioural approach for yourself first. See if it can help you handle your feelings about the bullying situation and enable you to model positive attitudes for your child. Then decide whether you want to explain to her how the technique works and help her to have a go.

You might find that my children's book, *How 2 B Happy* (A and C Black, 2006) will help your child explore CBT and some of the other ideas in these chapters through fun quizzes and stories.

Check, Challenge, Choose

Whenever you feel anxious or unhappy – stop. Check what thoughts are going through your head. Challenge those thoughts by asking: Are they true? Are they helpful? If they either aren't true or aren't making you happy, then choose a different way of looking at things. It's as easy as that.

For example, supposing your child didn't want to go to school but you made her go – that's always a tough call when bullying is an issue. As soon as you drop her at the school gates you might start feeling bad and as the day goes on, unless you do something about it, you'll probably just feel worse and worse. Feeling bad is the prompt you need to make you stop and check what you are thinking.

One thought might be, 'I shouldn't have made her go'. To challenge that thought you would need to ask if that is true. Can you be absolutely sure it's true? Although she might be having a horrible time at school, on the other hand, she might not. In fact, any number of positive things might be happening. For all you know, the bullies might have found someone else to pick on, your child might have started up a supportive new friendship or her teacher might have thought of an effective way to sort the problem out. It's also possible that your child could be having a eureka moment, realizing that just because people say nasty things it doesn't mean there's anything wrong with her.

Therefore, you can't be sure that 'I shouldn't have made her go' is true. The next thing to check is whether that thought is helpful. Does it make you feel happy? No – it makes you feel anxious and guilty.

So could you choose a better way of thinking about making your child go to school? Yes. You could choose to think that you have helped her face her demons and given her the opportunity to keep working with her problem instead of running away from it. You could say to yourself, 'I have given her firm guidance and shown her I believe she can cope'.

The result of this check-challenge-choose is that you will have a better day and this will mean you can be calmer when your child gets home. If it should turn out that she had a tough time and 'I shouldn't have made her go' kicks in again, you can use exactly the same process to deal with it as you did before. Is it true? Can you be absolutely sure? Well, yes, she had a bad day . . . but what if that proves to be the catalyst for change? Maybe her teacher noticed what was going on, maybe her friends felt bad about not sticking up for her and decided that they weren't going to stand by and let it happen again. You can't foresee all the consequences of the things you do.

Is 'I shouldn't have let her go' helpful now, in retrospect? No, because it means that all evening, instead of being a positive presence for your child, you'll be distracted by your own grief and guilt and worrying about what you're going to do when she doesn't want to go to school tomorrow.

'Should' flags up one sort of negative automatic response to experience which can creep in at times of stress, like when your child is being bullied. It can undermine your normally robust way of thinking or it can already be there, a strong undercurrent of guilt that has been part of the unconscious pattern of your early family life.

Whether they're already strong in you or gradually seeping in through difficult situations and events, these unhelpful ways of thinking are unconscious, and they will only come to light if you go looking for them. As it can help to know what you're looking for, here's a brief description of some of the most common cognitive distortions.

SOME COMMON COGNITIVE DISTORTIONS

'Should' Thinking

'Should' was one of the words the positive-thinking self-help books included as a negative, like 'difficult' and 'can't'. It didn't make a lot of sense to me because 'should' seemed actually quite positive, but I decided to try watching out for it anyway. In our family, we experimented with changing 'should' to 'could'. On one occasion, my youngest child told us at tea time, 'My teacher used the "sh" word in front of the whole class today!' We were momentarily agog.

'She said "shit"?' exclaimed her brother, scandalized.

She gave him a withering look. 'Of course she didn't, silly,' she said. 'Everyone knows the "sh" word is "should"!'

It's very interesting what happens when you start noticing 'should' or 'shouldn't' because you soon realize how it can become a sort of alternative to actually doing something. In relation to your child's situation you could think, 'This should-n't be happening', 'The other kids shouldn't be mean to my child', 'My child shouldn't let it get to her so much'. In an ideal world you might be right but in the real world it is happening, the other kids are being mean and your child is letting it get to her. 'Should' keeps you sitting there full of righteous indignation, feeling disappointed, resentful and bewildered; you can only rise to the challenge by letting go of how you think things should be and working out what you could do about it. That's changing 'should' to 'could'.

For example, if you feel your child shouldn't let it get to her you are rejecting the reality of her situation and that will make her feel worse as well as meaning that you won't be looking for ways to help her. By accepting that, whether you like it or not, she is feeling upset, you put yourself on her side. Then you are both looking for a solution together.

> Remember to watch out for 'should' in your self-talk too. 'I should be able to handle this better', 'I should be more supportive', 'I should be less protective'. Change 'should' to 'could' and that will push you automatically towards looking for practical solutions. 'I could be handling this better' – how? What could you do? Talk to a friend, maybe, and get some support for yourself. 'I could be more supportive', 'I could be less protective' – yes, and now you could think of some strategies.

'Should' keeps you passive in the present and can also lock you into past regrets. Supposing you think, 'I should have taken that other job'. Is that true? Can you be absolutely sure that it's true? Maybe the other job would have been very stressful or undemanding; maybe the office atmosphere wasn't as warm and positive as it seemed when you went for interview. Is 'I should have taken that other job' helpful? No, it makes you look back and feel sad. 'I could have taken that other job' means accepting the present reality – you could have, but you didn't.

When it comes to past mistakes, what could you do, realistically? You could say sorry and make amends, if what you did involved somebody else, and that's all – you can never undo something once it's done. Then you could forgive yourself and decide to learn from your mistake. Those are the real choices you've got; they're what you could do if you let go of 'should'.

If you feel you should have handled the meeting with your child's teacher better, well maybe you could have. So instead of beating yourself up about it, you could contact her again and apologize for losing your temper. You could ask for another meeting. Letting go of 'should' brings you back into the real world, where you can actually be effective.

Negative Focus

Worrying about all the bad things in life can easily make us lose our sense of proportion, and stop us noticing the good things. When a child is bullied, even though the bullying takes up only a tiny proportion of her day, she can become so obsessed by her unhappiness about being bullied that she loses sight of all the good things in her life.

There's a game that shows exactly how this works, and you might like to try it with your child next time she's feeling that her whole life is terrible.

Ask your child to look carefully around the room and notice anything that's red. Give her plenty of time. Then get her to close her eyes and tell you everything she can remember seeing that was blue.

She will probably say, 'I can't do it! You told me to look for red! What was the point in that?' The point is that if you're only looking at red you don't notice blue, and if you're only looking at what's bad you don't notice what's good.

Unfortunately, negative focus often kicks in at the very times when you need a clear awareness of the great things in life in order to help you get through. Your child needs that if she's being bullied, and so do you.

So think about how much you focus on your child's problems and how much on her joys. When she comes home from school, what do you talk about? If you don't talk much, what are you thinking, in relation to your child?

Also, noticing what you focus on in your own life will show you what kind of role model you are for her. When someone asks, 'How was your day?' do you normally launch into a list of grumbles or cherry-pick the good bits? Do you think of yourself as having had a bad life or a good life? If I were to ask you to write down the first five things you think of that happened last week, or in the past few years, or in your lifetime, would they be mostly positive or negative experiences?

You can feel what a difference your focus makes by writing a good day / bad day diary entry for yesterday. Do it first including all the irritating and difficult things that happened and leaving out the good ones. 'I couldn't get Hannah out of bed because she didn't want to go to school, and when she did eventually get up she wouldn't speak to me or eat any breakfast, and I could have done without the attitude because I was already running late . . .'

Then do another diary entry including only the good things and leaving out the bad. 'I managed to get Hannah off to school all right and arrived at work just in time . . .'

Positive focus isn't about denial – both the good day and the bad day are equally true – it's about choice. By becoming conscious of the choices we make, we are empowered to change them. Then we become the author of our own life stories, deciding for ourselves what to include and what to leave out, and therefore what kind of stories they are. If your story or your child's story has recently become sad or tragic it could be helpful to shift your focus and start concentrating more on the good things.

Besides only noticing the bad things, negative focus also includes two other distortions – discounting the positive and accentuating the negative. Discounting the positive is when you dismiss the good things you've got or done as unimportant – 'I've got an OK car, but who hasn't?' 'So I can cook – it's not exactly rocket science'. Accentuating the negative is when you exaggerate the importance of the bad things – 'I never make cakes and cookies – I must be a terrible mother!'

Emotional Reasoning

Emotional reasoning is when you take your emotions as evidence of how things really are, for example: 'I feel guilty therefore I must have done something wrong.' When your child is upset you might feel inadequate that you can't make everything OK, and with emotional reasoning you could think that feeling inadequate must prove that you are inadequate. If you check for evidence, it isn't true. The plain fact is that parents can't always make everything OK for their child, so you're not inadequate, you're normal.

Your child might feel extremely upset by teasing within her friendship group that is actually intended in fun, but with emotional reasoning she might think that as she's so upset the others must be trying to hurt her.

Emotions can run high in bullying situations and it's important not to let them colour the way you interpret and understand events.

All-Or-Nothing Thinking

You can easily spot all-or-nothing thinking by its telltale signs – 'nothing', 'never', 'nobody' – and children who are bullied are particularly prone to it. Sooner or later almost every bullied child will say things like 'Nobody likes me' and 'It's never going to stop' and 'There's nothing I can do'. Other words that flag up all-or-nothing thinking are 'everything', 'always' and 'everybody' as in 'Everybody hates me'.

All-or-nothing thinking is very destructive because it acts like a magnet to negative experiences. For example, say your local council wants to build a car park on the field next to you. If you think, 'There's nothing I can do about it, nobody will listen, they never take any notice of people like me', then you probably won't even try to stop it happening. If you don't try your chance of success is zero. At least if you think you can do something you will want to try, and that's all you need in order to have a chance of success.

Supposing you tell your child off and she thinks, 'Mum's always having a go at me' and 'I never do anything right'. That thought will make her want to play up, and then you'll have to tell her off again, which will reinforce the idea that you're always having a go – a cycle that keeps delivering negative experience for everybody.

As with other cognitive distortions, all-or-nothing thinking doesn't stand up to scrutiny – it isn't true, it isn't helpful and it falls apart as soon as you question it. If you think 'My child is always being picked on' and so on, notice all the times that other people either leave her alone or are actually nice to her. If you think she hasn't got any friends, notice all the people who really care about her. They may not be in her school peer group, but they are still someone – they still exist. Help her to notice that there's always 'sometimes, something, somebody' however bleak things might be feeling.

Whenever you spot all-or-nothing thinking in your attitudes

towards the bullying situation or anything else, letting go of it will mean you'll be setting a great example for your child as well as increasing your own chance of happiness and success.

Pessimism

If you grow up with pessimistic attitudes you can feel they're sensible and realistic, but they aren't. Nobody can tell what's going to happen in the future. It makes no more sense to anticipate bad things than good and, in fact, it's much more sensible to expect the best because optimists enjoy better health and live longer than pessimists – true!

A lot of people expect the worst in every situation because they are trying to protect themselves from being disappointed. This obviously doesn't work because even someone who expects the worst will still be disappointed when things go wrong. Sometimes they might try to protect their children too, by warning them that they should be prepared for trouble and setbacks, instead of encouraging them to assume everything will be fine.

If you always expect the best you can live in a state of pleasurable anticipation, whereas if you expect the worst your life is overshadowed by anxiety and dread.

Consider Jane's story:

Jane

Jane was on a camping weekend with her family, and on the very first evening she noticed she'd lost the ring her grandmother gave her. Her husband and children searched high and low, but there was no sign of the ring.

Her husband took the view that the ring would show up if it was meant to, and if it was lost then there was nothing anyone could do about it anyway.

Jane was distraught. She was angry with her husband for making light of her loss, and spent the whole weekend fretting over it.

Which one would you rather be, Jane or her husband? Which one would you rather live with?

This isn't my story, but it's a true story, so I can tell you what happened in the end. When they took the tent down Jane found her ring on the flattened grass underneath the ground-sheet.

So when your child leaves the house in the morning full of anticipation and dread, don't pay into it. Expect her to cope well and enjoy herself. That way you will not only be freeing yourself to get on with the business of the day without worrying about her all the time, you will also be freeing her from the additional burden of responsibility for upsetting you. As well as that, you will be modelling a much more robust approach to life, which will inevitably begin to rub off on her.

If you always anticipate the best, you're twice a winner. You not only enjoy a much better quality of life, not worrying about what the future might bring, you will also have a positive effect on what the future does bring.

A friend of mine, for instance, hates her birthdays. She always expects them to be miserable, and they always are. Another friend loves hers. She expects to enjoy them, and she does.

Illusion of Control

Expecting the worst is one way we try to protect ourselves against future catastrophe; the illusion of control is another. We think that if we can just get the right information and take the right action, we can control what happens to us.

This idea underpins our addiction to the news media that bombards us with frightening scenarios and spices them up by suggesting they're much more likely to affect us personally than they really are. We think it's sensible to avoid going into hospital in case we get an infection, to stay at home in case we get blown up by terrorists and to stop enjoying soft cheese in case we get listeria.

Even when a risk is real on the individual level, the idea that we can manipulate the future is still an illusion. We might try to avoid heart disease by cutting down on cholesterol only to get cancer instead, from eating too much hydrogenated vegetable oil; we might try to avoid unemployment by working hard only to find we've become too experienced and too expensive to be employable.

Trying to manipulate the future is not only a waste of time, it's also very tiring. It uses up energy that could be employed better in enjoying the present. It can be a wonderful release just to let it go.

Accepting what happens when it happens is a much less frustrating and anxious way of living. It's an attitude that can grow from the most trivial incidents to have a profound effect on your whole experience of life.

I remember a few years ago, going down to south Cornwall

for the day. The weather was good for early spring, and we walked for miles along the coastal footpath. When we got back to the car we were all really hungry so we drove into Marazion to look for a café. We found the perfect place, but just as we were about to go in, the 'Closed' sign went up.

It was half past four in the afternoon. We could have felt annoyed, frustrated, despondent, but we decided to trust the process. We had just set off for home when we noticed a take-away pizza place overlooking the bay. We sat out eating pizzas on the beach, watching the sun go down. It wasn't what we had planned – it was actually better.

> Giving up the illusion of control means accepting that there will be setbacks as well as successes. It means acknowledging that as we can't tell what the future will bring we can't judge our present experience as 'good' or 'bad'. What looks like a problem today – say, you didn't get the job you wanted – could turn out tomorrow to have been a blessing when you get an even better one.

CREATING A POSITIVE ENVIRONMENT

Both positive thinking and CBT propose that your quality of life doesn't depend on what happens to you but on the way you respond to experience. Most of the time, you aren't even aware of the automatic attitudes that determine how you see things, whether they come from your culture, early family situation or formative life events. As long as these attitudes are unconscious you have no control over them.

By becoming aware of your automatic responses you can gain some mastery over your life, but if you also try out different ways of looking at things and choose for yourself the ones that work best, then you are taking control and creating the life you want.

A particularly good time to test these thought patterns is when your child is being bullied, because it is in stressful situations that negative thinking patterns are most likely to kick in.

When you first try to replace unhelpful thoughts with positive ones you might experience resistance from people around you because you are breaking the mould. If your friendship group is bonded by negative focus, where you all like to have a good grumble, the others might not take kindly to you suddenly looking on the bright side. They might even experience it as an affront. Say one starts complaining about her husband and then another one joins in, and then a third – what will they make of it when you only want to focus on the good things about yours?

If your family favours 'should' thinking and you say you're going to buy a few self-help books for your child to help her deal with teasing, your parents might think you've lost the plot and protest, 'She shouldn't have to deal with it herself. The school should sort it out!'

If your child is stuck in all-or-nothing thinking and you're trying to get her to notice that some people like her and some things go OK and sometimes she actually has a good day at school, she might accuse you of patronizing her or not taking her problems seriously.

As well as coming up against resistance in other people you might also experience strong resistance within yourself when you're trying to let go of negative attitudes. This isn't just because negative thinking can be a habit as hard to break as any other bad habit. It's also because there are significant hidden advantages in seeing yourself as a victim of circumstances rather than someone who has the power to create the life they want.

For a start, you get sympathy from other people. Poor you – all these horrible things keep happening! In fact, sometimes, the less well you cope the more sympathy you get. Playing on people's sympathy means you can get out of doing things too – 'I'm sorry, I'm just too upset to go to the PTA meeting', 'I can't help out at the Brownies' barbecue when I've got all these problems to deal with'.

It's also less stressful being a negative thinker. If you expect the worst and don't even try then there's absolutely no risk of failure, and if you get knocked down it's much easier to stay down than try to pick yourself up again.

Not taking responsibility for creating your own life means you can just sit back and blame everybody else, as in, 'I'd be fine if my daughter wasn't so strung out or those kids stopped bullying her or the school did something about it . . .'

For your child, one hidden advantage of negative thinking

is that it will make her unhappy, and unhappy people aren't a threat to anyone. If she were to be as happy, successful and positive as she could possibly be then people might feel jealous and try to spoil things for her. If she stays gloomy, they don't have to bother because she's already doing their work for them.

If you feel a strong resistance within yourself when you are working on developing positive attitudes it can be helpful to externalize that critical inner voice. Imagine what it would look like if you could take it out and see it. What would it be saying to you? When I did this, I found it was like a fierce little hobgoblin in a hole, and he was saying 'Get lost! Leave me alone! I can be miserable if I want to!'

When you create a visual image for your resistance, you can deal with it more easily. You can have a dialogue. Maybe I want to try a new hobby and my hobgoblin pipes up, 'What's the point? You won't be any good at it!' Then I can hear my own negative thought and argue against it. 'How do you know? I might be brilliant!'

Trying to become aware of your automatic thoughts in response to experience and then trying alternatives is, at the very least, an interesting experiment. At best it could be a revelation for you as it was for me, and knowing that you can create the life you want no matter what happens to you is a brilliant attitude to model for your bullied child.

RECAP POINTS

- Bullying feels like a disaster and if the situation persists you and your child can get bogged down by negative and catastrophic thoughts
- Positive thinking can be an effective antidote
- A cognitive approach can help you notice negative thoughts and challenge them
- Choosing positive attitudes will help you and your child to feel calmer and more able to cope

CHAPTER FIVE

Holding on to Happiness

One of the most distressing things about having a child who is being bullied is watching his happiness, enthusiasm and general *joie de vivre* drain away. The misery from bullying doesn't stay inside the school gates; it follows him everywhere and infects every part of his life. Your bullied child's unhappiness makes you unhappy too, and that makes your other children unhappy, and so the misery can spread.

Unhappiness saps your energy and makes you less able to cope with the vicissitudes of life. Various experiments in kinaesthesiology have shown that your muscle power is actually affected by how you feel. Bad feelings make you weaker; good feelings make you strong. If you want to build up your child's physical stature and presence and help him to have more assertive body language, an injection of happy feelings will be every bit as effective as those self-defence lessons that most bullying books recommend, and many bullied children shrink from in horror.

> You can help your child to hold on to his happiness, even though he's being bullied, by simply holding on to your own, because feeling happy will give you the strength to develop the sort of family situation that actively promotes feelings of wellbeing and optimism rather than apathy and despondency.

This is not to say that you, your child or anyone else in the world can hope to be happy 24/7. In fact, the crucial first step in maximizing the happiness in your life is a robust acceptance that sometimes everybody is bound to feel unhappy. One of the causes of our modern epidemic of depression is the myth that if we aren't happy all the time there must be something wrong with us. This leaves us prone to compounding our unhappiness with anxiety about our mental health and a sense of personal failure.

Expecting a child who is being bullied to feel happy all the time would be to place an extra burden on him – but helping him to feel happy more of the time will give him reserves to draw upon to stop bullying getting him down.

THE SCIENCE OF HAPPINESS

The idea behind traditional psychology is that if you can root out the reasons for unhappy feelings you can cure them by a sort of catharsis, but although this may work in some cases its success rate is limited and not improving. However, the thinking behind the relatively new 'positive psychology' is that traditional therapy is backward-looking, focused entirely on negative emotions and experiences that can make people feel more helpless, confused and despondent than they were to start with. Positive psychologists have called the traditional approach 'victimology'.

Over the last forty years therapists such as Abraham Maslow and Martin Seligman have been working with creative and forward-looking theories, trying to help clients to activate the positive rather than delve endlessly into what's gone wrong, but these ideas are only now moving into the mainstream.

Positive psychology is trying to apply the rigours of science to an approach based on promoting good feelings rather than just trying to cure bad ones, on looking at ways of increasing happiness so that negative feelings are less able to take hold. High-profile research into what makes people happy rather than unhappy has been hitting the news, raising awareness and sparking public debate.

Positive psychologists believe that difficult emotions are natural and even important to our survival and growth, and therefore it isn't pragmatic or even desirable to try to eradicate them. Because everyone has problems and setbacks, everyone is bound to experience unhappiness, but that can actually be a positive thing. Emotional pain, like physical pain, is essential to our health and survival.

People who are unable to feel pain can be in danger, as I know from my own childhood. My father suffered from multiple sclerosis and had little feeling in his hands and feet. On one occasion, his hand was resting on the electric hob and he didn't realize the hot plate was switched on until he smelled his skin burning.

As physical pain is an early warning that can protect you from serious harm, so emotional pain also has positive, protective functions. Supposing you made a mistake and felt really stupid – you wouldn't do the same thing again because you wouldn't want to experience the same feeling. What's more, the pain of feeling foolish would spur you on to try something else instead next time and so increase your understanding.

Supposing you had the chance to meet one of your heroes but you hung back out of shyness and lack of confidence. You would feel really frustrated with yourself, and that horrible feeling might ensure that the next time you got such an opportunity you wouldn't let it slip through your fingers again.

Starting from the assumption that we need negative emotions for our survival and growth, positive psychologists look for ways of enabling people to cope better with the bad times by boosting the general level of happiness in their life. This takes effort and daily practice because happiness does not come naturally to all people at all times.

You can start the work of happiness-building straight away by trying some of the techniques that research has shown to be successful. The first thing to think about is cultivating positive emotions.

POSITIVE EMOTIONS

You don't have to wait for positive emotions to come along – you can actively set out to cultivate them in your life. Probably the easiest one to begin with is gratitude.

Gratitude

The positive effects of gratitude are well documented and they aren't only emotional. Gratitude has been shown to have surprising and measurable effects upon the body as well. Dr Paul Brand, in his book, *Pain: The Gift Nobody Wants – A Surgeon's Journey of Discovery* (Marshall Pickering, 1993), describes how, after a lifetime working on understanding pain, he came to prescribe gratitude as the most powerful painkiller and the best protection against disease.

Here are three ideas for getting more gratitude into your life.

One: Every night before you go to sleep, think of five things that you're glad to have in your life and say thank you. Thank you for my child, thank you for my partner, thank you for my new shoes, thank you for the wonderful gift of chocolate . . .

They don't have to be huge, important things – in fact, practising gratitude can be a great way of drawing your attention to just how wonderful even the smallest things are. Saying thank you helps to focus your attention on the positive aspects of your life and is an effective antidote to the modern-day pressure to want what we haven't got instead of appreciating what we have.

If you don't try a single other idea in this book, please have a go at this one. It's so quick and simple, but when you make it part of your daily practice, the effects can be truly profound.

Two: Think of a person who has been a great help or support to you at some time in your life and write them a thank-you letter. Explain how important they were and what a difference it made to you having them around.

Simply writing this letter will give you the experience of feeling grateful, but if you have an address for the person, don't be shy about sending it. Give them a good reason to feel grateful too.

Three: Have a thankful meal with family or friends. Start the first course by going round the table with each person saying thank you for something to the person on their left – 'Thank you for listening when I felt fed up last week', 'Thank you for lending me your lawn-mower', 'Thank you for looking so bright and smiley'.

Start the second course doing the same thing going in the opposite direction, with everyone thanking the person on their right.

Start the third course or finish up with a round of general gratitude, sharing the things you really appreciate about life in general.

Everyone has got something to feel grateful for and the more you practise gratitude the easier it gets because your awareness of the good things grows.

In the fullness of time it may even be possible to feel grateful for the painful things, the gifts nobody wants, and that's where gratitude links to another positive feeling that's worth cultivating – a sense of purpose.

A Sense of Purpose

Problems push you outside your comfort zone, so that you have to develop new skills in order to deal with them, and that's why every problem is an opportunity for growth. Little problems are opportunities for a little growth, and big ones are opportunities for major growth.

Treating problems as opportunities is the best way to take the sting out of them because then you are introducing a sense of purpose, which feels very positive, and that will counterbalance the emotional pain, making it easier to manage.

The easiest way to start practising a sense of purpose is with little setbacks and problems, noticing how they challenge you and help you to grow.

Supposing you can't get any books by your favourite authors at the library: if you accept the opportunity and don't just go home in disgust, this could be a chance for you to extend yourself by trying some different writers.

Supposing your friend drops out at the last minute and you have to go to your new evening class on your own: you might feel nervous, disappointed, angry – you might even decide not to go. But this setback is also an opportunity because it means that instead of playing safe within the shelter of an established friendship you will have to introduce yourself to people you don't know and make new friends.

Every problem is a chance to make your life bigger – without problems to challenge you your life would stay the same. Noticing the benefits that can come from small problems can help you to see there is positive potential in bigger ones.

Being bullied might be a very big problem for you and your child, and that means it's a big opportunity. Many famous and successful people say that being bullied at school taught them the toughness and unshakable self-belief not only to succeed but also to cope with the pressures of success, such as bad press and rumour campaigns. When the going gets tough, as the saying goes, the tough get going.

Some examples are:

- Top singer Darius – he was completely slated by the judges in *Pop Idol* but came back to great acclaim the following year
- Charlotte Church – she was teased for having less money than her classmates in Cardiff (who's laughing now?)
- Tom Cruise – he had a learning problem
- Mel Gibson – he was chubby and spoke with a different accent
  Sarah Cox, David Beckham, Orlando Bloom, Christina Aguilera, Frank Bruno . . . the list is endless.

Nobody wants to have problems but you can soften the blow by seeing them as opportunities – that's positive psychology. Developing a sense of purpose means accepting the challenge of negative experience in order to push back your boundaries and realize your full potential.

Love

The more you love the happier you feel and it doesn't matter what or who is the object of your love. Try this little experiment to test the positive power of love.

Take any object that has no emotional significance to you. It might be a table, for example. Look at it for a while. Think: I love you, table! Notice how you feel, and any physical response. Now tell that table out loud, 'I love you, table!'

What you feel is your own love energy reflected back. It seems ridiculous, but loving even a table can make your skin tingle and bring a smile to your face. If you try it on something more sophisticated, like your computer or your car, you might be surprised by the result.

The car we used to drive went like a dream in the dry weather, but it didn't like the damp and we were resigned to the fact that there would be several wet mornings every year when we'd just have to get a taxi to take the children to school.

Then, one dismal October day, when the car wouldn't start, one of the children suggested we try a bit of positive love energy. I thought it was rather a long shot, but I got back in and we all began to love the car! Instead of frustration and fury, we gave gratitude for all the times it had started and got us to school; instead of slams and kicks we gave a calming touch.

The immediate effect on all of us was brilliant. The tension and anxiety evaporated, and we were able to accept the situation and feel OK about it. The effect on the car was astonishing! It started on the very next try. Once we had decided to adopt a loving attitude towards the car, we never had to get a taxi again.

I've found exactly the same thing with my computer. If it starts playing up, instead of spending hours battling with it and getting more and more angry and frustrated like I used to, I just switch it off and give us both time to calm down. I usually find my computer works fine again when I come back to it in a more positive frame of mind.

I had a watch that liked to take a rest too – it used to stop whenever I went on holiday. The first few times it happened I thought the battery had run out, so I got it checked but the battery was fine. Then as soon as I got home, hey presto, my watch would start working again. It made me laugh and I felt quite tickled to be so in tune with my timepiece.

My daughter overcame her fear of certain no-go areas in her school by telling them, as she passed through, 'I love you, corridors!' Doubtless her body language became more assertive and self-assured, so as well as experiencing the corridors as less threatening she probably reduced any actual threat to herself. Feeling nervous and uneasy is the best way to attract the attention of people who are looking for someone to intimidate.

Practising positive love on things, where you don't need to worry about what sort of reaction you might get, is excellent preparation for practising it on people. The table hasn't done anything to deserve your love, and it won't do anything to return it; the joy of loving is your gift, which is simply reflected back to you in good feelings.

You can choose to love people in the same unconditional way, purely for the joy of loving, and because it doesn't depend on getting anything back you can practise any time you like.

*

As well as cultivating happy emotions in the present, you can consciously work on feeling happy about the past and the future. You can choose to look back with feelings of pride, satisfaction and serenity, and to face the future in a spirit of optimism, trust and faith.

HAPPY ACTIVITIES

As well as cultivating positive emotions as a buffer against hard times, you can boost your happiness by including certain sorts of activity in your everyday life. Particularly beneficial are things that give you the experience of 'flow'.

The Experience of 'Flow'

What positive psychologists mean by 'flow' is the feeling you get when you are so completely absorbed in something that you lose all sense of time and forget about your worries and concerns. Everyone has to find their own experience of flow by following what has heart and meaning for them, because there's no one-size-fits-all formula. Maybe gardening takes you out of yourself, or walking, or cross-stitch, or painting, or cooking, or sport.

This is worth thinking about because there seems to be a direct link between how much you experience flow and how happy you are generally in life. Yet often in times of stress people sideline the very activities that could nurture them most because they simply don't realize how important they are. Flow activities can help you stay afloat when you're most in danger of going under.

You need flow activities to energize and refresh you so that you can achieve well in the things you have to do. Prioritizing work over everything else, which starts in the education system and runs through the whole of modern society, doesn't only mean we miss out on fun things but also that we actually don't work as efficiently.

If you haven't got many flow activities this could be a good time to go looking for some; if you have, hold on to them, and increase the time you spend on them if you can. Encourage your child to do the same.

You can free up some time by doing something else that has been shown to increase happiness – cutting down on TV.

Cutting Down on TV

I'm a great fan of television – I think it can be informative and fun. But it can also become addictive and take over your family life if you aren't careful.

You can take control and maximize the benefits of TV by being more selective about what you watch. Some programmes can have a marked effect on your mood and outlook. Dramas and documentaries about hideous diseases, vicious wars, political corruption and violent crime – and, of course, news bulletins – will not help anyone develop a balanced and optimistic outlook. Game shows, reality TV shows and the sort of comedy programmes that humiliate people also demean viewers by encouraging them to laugh at someone else's discomfort.

Comedies, natural history programmes, adventure stories and dramas, on the other hand, can make you feel happy, relaxed or pleasantly excited. A counsellor friend of mine recommends to all her clients a daily dose of something they find funny on television. Watching half an hour of comedy with your family – anything that makes you all smile – will lift your spirits and bring you together.

You might like to try moving away from violent and depressing television programmes altogether for a week or two. It could feel odd at first, and even perhaps trivial, given the inflated value we place on so-called 'information'. But it's only when you stop watching these programmes that you notice how much gloom and anxiety they generate, and they quickly lose their appeal.

Television itself becomes less of an addiction and more of a choice when you use it in this more selective way. To start, get a TV guide at the beginning of the week and circle the programmes you *really* want to watch. Between programmes, turn the TV off.

If you're worried about filling in the gaps, here are some more tried-and-tested happy activities.

Exercise

Research shows that physical exercise can boost levels of the feel-good chemical serotonin as much as antidepressants, and some doctors are now prescribing exercise instead of drugs. As well as being an effective treatment, its only side effects are beneficial – better health and fitness.

The ideal exercise for you will be something that gives you the flow experience. If you're the sort of person who loves targets and timetables you might enjoy going to the gym but if you aren't there's no need to complicate exercise with science. If you're a sociable sort who likes to be part of a team, then something like football or netball could be better for you, but it wouldn't be much good for someone who prefers the calm concentration of yoga.

When you're thinking about factoring in some exercise as a way of nurturing happiness, the only thing you need to focus on is enjoyment. The health benefits are a side effect, so don't think in terms of how many calories you're going to burn, or how much fat you can convert into muscle – think of it in terms of how keen you are to do it.

For a lot of people a walk around the neighbourhood or a bit of gardening can be hard to beat. You can do these things any time you like, alone or in company, and they have the added advantage of being out of doors in natural daylight.

Nature

There's a whole science of ecopsychology, which studies the link between the natural environment and individual wellbeing, and now positive psychologists have found that nature is indeed a boost to happiness.

There are lots of ways you can enjoy the benefits of nature without necessarily getting right out into the countryside. Walking in a park or down a leafy suburban street will do, or sitting in your garden. Growing things is another way of enjoying the slow rhythms of nature – window boxes and patio tubs will do if you haven't got a garden, and house plants can be a soothing presence in the home.

Even pictures of the natural world can be a way of bringing nature inside, and remember that nature includes animals as well as plants. One of the things that can bring immense pleasure into your life is a pet because a dog or cat or rabbit is a little piece of nature brought inside.

Laughter

Smiles and laughter boost the serotonin level in your brain – even if you're faking it – and a good laugh has the added benefit of giving a boost to the immune system so it'll be helping to keep your family healthy too.

You don't have to take up laughter yoga (yes, this really exists) or have a course in laughter therapy (so does this) – you can raise a smile by remembering something nice, or have a chuckle thinking about something funny. Simply smiling more at other people will make a difference.

Watching comedy films, playing amusing board games, telling jokes and generally larking around together is all good stuff for your family life – but be a little wary of teasing. Sometimes people can laugh but be hurt inside, and teasing that is kindly meant can undermine a person's self-image. As a general rule, don't say anything in a jokey way that you would not say in a serious voice – concentrate on the words rather than the tone when you're thinking about what's acceptable. Your child might be as thin as a beanpole so if you say something like,

'Shift up, you lardy lump!' you would obviously be being ironic, but it might not feel funny to him.

Conversation

Talking to people is a great happiness boost but in today's frenetic world sometimes it gets a very low priority after work, household chores, TV and just about everything else.

If a family sits down and eats together without the TV on at least once a week this doesn't only create better relationships, it also seems to make a significant difference to children's school performance. Communicating with each other means sharing experiences and discussing ideas and just generally showing concern, even if it sometimes involves disagreements.

> For maximum happiness, try to have at least one proper sustained conversation every day. Your children might not manage more than ten minutes or so, but that's worth gold dust, so go for it anyway. For a longer chat, have a glass of wine with your partner, a gossip with your neighbour, a telephone catch-up with a friend – it doesn't matter who you talk to so long as you talk.

At the risk of stating the exceedingly obvious, and just because I spent half an hour stuck in a car this morning with someone who hardly stopped talking to draw breath, please remember that a conversation is 50 per cent talking and 50 per cent listening!

Learning

Lots of people who have given up on learning because they didn't much enjoy it at school are amazed to find, in adult life, that taking classes in something they're interested in can give them a fantastic buzz. In one piece of research, more than half of the adult learners interviewed said that they found learning more enjoyable than sex!

An evening class can provide you with time out, new acquaintances and possibly even the experience of flow. Recent government initiatives mean that classes available at your local secondary school are likely to be more weighted towards academic subjects that lead to a qualification than more practical or adventurous ones like dry-stone walling, martial arts, assertiveness training and so on. Your local library will have information on classes offered privately, your health shop might have some for more alternative subjects and you could watch out in your local newspaper 'What's On' as well.

If you're interested in sport, you could enquire what's on offer at leisure centres in your area, or if you're interested in drama check out theatres and theatrical groups. You can get informal learning experiences in book groups or knitting circles, where you get together with friends in order to share an interest or activity. This doesn't have to be a regular thing. You can organize one-offs or occasional evenings based around a theme, where each person brings their favourite piece of music to listen to and share, for example, or their favourite picture or poem.

Even following an interest on your own means you are extending your knowledge and understanding, and the happiness dividend can be just as great.

The best way to find the learning that will make you happiest is to approach it with happiness as your only goal and not worry about things like 'Is it important?' and 'Is it useful?' If you take your classes or do your researches for the sheer joy of it, this will also be giving your child very positive messages about the value you place on both pleasure and learning, and it might inspire him to pursue his own interests in the same happiness-nurturing spirit.

Stillness

Einstein said there are only two ways to live your life – as if everything is a miracle or as if nothing is. Actually, if you take time out to really notice what's all around you, I think there's only one way.

Busy, busy, busy isn't a recipe for happiness, yet that's the way many of us live and the example we set for our children. Slow down. Try taking a few seconds out at least once a day for a miracle moment. Whenever you remember to, stop what you're doing and look around. Choose one thing you can see and focus all your attention on it – a sandwich, an orange curtain, a cat on a wall, your mobile phone . . . Notice its colours and textures, every tiny detail of its appearance. Does it make any sounds? Think about where it came from, how it was made, the human dimension and the material. Everything is amazing to anyone who simply takes the time to notice.

A miracle moment is like a mini meditation, a flow experience that takes you outside of yourself, off the treadmill of your normal thoughts and assumptions. It's a drop of stillness, and stillness is good for the body, heart and mind. Miracle moments tend to proliferate – when you start to notice the mundane things in this way, it's a small step to extending the pleasure into, say, five minutes just watching the birds on your bird table or sitting quietly turning a pebble over in your hands.

Introducing more stillness into your life means you will feel less stressed and be less likely to put pressure on your child – pressure he can do without when he's dealing with bullying. It will encourage him to value restfulness and not feel bad about 'wasting time' by just messing around, daydreaming and giving himself time to appreciate the small things in life.

As you experiment with these activities that positive psychologists recommend, think also about your own particular lifestyle. Does the food you eat make you feel good? Do the colours you surround yourself with make you feel cheerful and strong? Do you have enough music in your life? Enough silence? And what about the wonderful power of perfume to evoke moods of calmness or exhilaration?

Do the people you mix with make you feel happy or gloomy? My yoga teacher used to talk about people being radiators or drains – some will enthuse, comfort and invigorate you with their warm energy, but others will bring you down and leave you feeling drained. Nobody's jolly all the time and you wouldn't want to abandon a friend who's going through a crisis, but spending lots of time with people who seem to make it their life's work to complain and feel gloomy will only bring you down. If you want to be happy, find radiators and keep away from drains!

All this positive action on the home front can bring you to a celebrational style of living that will nurture your inner strength and help your child to hold on to his happiness so that bullying can't take it all away.

CELEBRATION

Having a celebration is a great way of noticing and maximizing the good things in life. Normally, we think of celebrating only on specific dates like birthdays and anniversaries, or in response to a big event like getting a promotion or moving into a new house. But you can make celebration part of your everyday practice by turning this on its head – decide that you want to celebrate and then look around for reasons why.

Everyone has something to celebrate all the time, as you will notice when you cultivate more gratitude in your life and enjoy more miracle moments – so simply celebrate your blessings. Today, the sun is shining, I am alive, I can see and hear and touch and smell and taste – this calls for a celebration!

As well as your blessings you can celebrate your successes. They don't have to be huge public things like getting an OBE or winning the lottery – your personal successes could include getting the children to school on time, resisting that second doughnut or managing to reverse-park at the first attempt.

For bullied children, simply having the courage to go to school can be a triumph; for their parents, holding back from physically assaulting the children who are bullying them could be a triumph too.

A celebration doesn't have to be a huge affair. A party with cake and champagne might be great for your happiness from time to time, but a simple family celebration – a day trip or a special meal – can be just as good, and so can an individual celebration such as a treat for your child or flowers for your partner.

Celebration can be private and personal too, and giving yourself a little treat every day is one way of boosting your general happiness. If you can't think of anything to do, consider ways of pleasing your five senses. A warm soak in an aromatic bath, a cup of coffee in your favourite café, ten minutes in an easy chair with Mozart . . .

Actually having a personal celebration could itself be something to celebrate if you're normally more comfortable putting everybody else first. But the more you practise celebration the less you will need to find a reason for it because the pleasure it brings into your life will be reason enough.

Pleasure is important because it contributes to your general happiness. No one can be happy all the time and when bad things happen everyone can be knocked down. But you don't have to stay down, and how well you bounce back will partly depend upon how much happiness you've got in the rest of your life to cushion your fall.

Your happiness and wellbeing is part of your child's cushion. When he is being bullied the best thing you can do for him is to hold on to your happiness so that you don't fall apart and add to his burden of misery with your own.

He can't feel happy during the seconds and minutes when he's actually being picked on, but he doesn't have to let that unhappiness take over his whole life. Being happy is a way of being strong and, especially in bullying situations, happiness is the best revenge.

RECAP POINTS

- Bullying can make both you and your child feel miserable, and feeling unhappy makes you weak
- You can draw on the findings of positive psychology to boost your happiness levels and create a buffer against bad times
- Cultivating more positive emotions and happy activities in your life will help you get through and provide a strong role model for your child

CHAPTER SIX

Building Self-esteem

People who are persistently bullied are likely to suffer from low self-esteem, and people with low self-esteem are more likely to be bullied. It's a vicious circle. The fact is, you can't defend yourself effectively if you don't think you're worth defending.

It's a very painful thing for parents of children who are being bullied to see their child become more and more self-conscious and self-rejecting. It's also very puzzling, because how can a child who is so loved and lovable fail to love herself?

The usual advice to parents is to tell your child as often as possible that she's wonderful and that you love her. This certainly won't do any harm but, according to experts, bullied children often have unusually close and loving family relationships anyway, so telling your child that you love her certainly can't be the whole answer.

Real self-esteem has to be grounded in real life and, like happiness, it can require effort and practice to establish and maintain, especially in times of stress.

SELF-ESTEEM FACTS AND FICTIONS

Some people are naturally more self-deprecating than others, and some more self-assured. Arguably, self-esteem might on occasion be considered a feature of temperament, with low self-esteem being associated with introspective, soulful, self-questioning personality types and high self-esteem with more outgoing ones. Family and social attitudes also play a big part in how self-esteem develops.

Your level of self-esteem is not set in stone, however, and it will fluctuate depending on circumstances. A big success can boost even the most diffident person's self-esteem. Bullying, if it goes on for long enough, is vicious enough or comes at a vulnerable time, can dent even the most confident child's self-esteem, and not being able to make it all better can dent any parent's.

High self-esteem doesn't depend on what you look like – you can be as plain as porridge and still feel fine about yourself. It doesn't depend on how much money you've got, either, or how clever you are. All you need in order to improve your self-esteem is to make the decision and do the work.

Puffing yourself up with big ideas about yourself and your abilities is not the way to do it because that will only give you false self-esteem, and false self-esteem is to real self-esteem as political spin is to real policy and achievement – everybody else can see right through it, and in the end it will all come tumbling down.

You can see false self-esteem at its most cringe-making on TV talent shows, where people who truly feel they have extraordinary gifts open themselves up to ridicule in auditions because it's obvious they aren't talented. False self-esteem is about illusions – real self-esteem is about knowing who you really are, including all your faults and failings, and still feeling good about yourself.

The other flaw in false self-esteem is that it takes no account of other people – all that matters is 'I'm the best'. Real self-esteem includes liking and respecting other people as much as you like and respect yourself.

Because the social aspect of building self-esteem is so often overlooked, I'm going to start with it in this chapter, and look at feeling comfortable within oneself in the next one.

The cornerstone of healthy social relationships is good boundaries and you can help your child to have a strong sense of herself, separate from everyone else and yet part of a social framework, by establishing good boundaries at home.

GOOD BOUNDARIES

Making good boundaries is important and easy. Here are some basic points.

Allow Privacy

Ideally, everybody should have somewhere they can go to be alone. If your child has her own room, allow her to lock it, or to put up a 'Do Not Disturb' notice that will be honoured. If she doesn't have her own room it will be doubly important to respect her need to be alone sometimes if she requests it.

All children who are old enough to unlock the bathroom door are old enough to lock it, and after the age of about seven or eight most children will not need help with bathing and hair-washing.

As well as physical privacy, we all need the privacy of our own thoughts. Heart-to-hearts are fine so long as no one feels pressurized to say more than they want to, and it should be taken for granted that nobody will listen in to telephone conversations, open letters or read diaries belonging to somebody else.

Finally, it's a good idea for everybody in the family to have a private life, separate from other family members – places you go, people you know, things you do that your partner and children don't join in with. For your child, growing up involves developing areas of experience she can gradually move into on her own, and seeing that you have these will help her to develop them too.

Encourage Differences

Your child needs to have her own views, develop her own tastes and make her own choices. Don't discourage this by criticizing her clothes, music, friends and so on; on the other hand, don't stifle it by taking over. As soon as you share her interest, it isn't her interest any more. If you are friends with her friends, they aren't her friends any more.

It's great to have some common interests, but if you identify too strongly with your child it will be much harder for her to get a strong sense of herself.

Let Everyone be Responsible for Themselves

If your two-year-old puts your auntie's pet poodle down the toilet when she's having tea with you, you might feel it's your responsibility. But as your children grow, they need to take responsibility for themselves. As far as possible, let them make their own decisions and take the consequences.

What if your child has a pet and she isn't remembering to check it has enough food and water every day? You might feel, on humanitarian grounds, that you should do it for her. But if she's old enough to have a pet, she's old enough to look after it. Make sure she knows the consequences of her pet being neglected in terms of suffering and ill-health, and warn her that if she doesn't look after it properly the consequence to her will be that she'll have to give it away to someone else who will. Whatever you do, don't let yourself be drawn into looking after it for her.

Letting your child take responsibility can sometimes be unnerving, When my youngest child was six I found her trying to peel and slice a raw carrot with a sharp knife to put in her packed lunch. I told her off and took away the knife. She took it back.

'A positive parent doesn't do anything for a child that the child can do for herself,' she told me, quoting word for word what I had said when refusing to tie her shoelaces for her the previous day. I showed her how to use a peeler, and forced myself to stand back and let her get on with it. You can always offer advice and support, but don't take more responsibility than you have to, depending on the age of the child.

In the same way, don't make other people responsible for your choices, either the major ones like the classic 'staying together for the sake of the children' or everyday things like not going out 'because I knew you wouldn't want me to'.

Maintain a Generation Gap

Adults have more power than children and that is a good thing for your child. She needs you to be in control as a grown-up so that she can see how to take control herself. She needs firm guidelines. It doesn't matter if your child agrees with your standards or not; seeing that you have standards and that you are able to maintain them will enable her to set her own as she grows up.

The standards you set at home will help your child to understand about rules, rights and responsibilities in the wider social context, and this will make her feel more confident about relating to other people and taking her place in the world.

RULES, RIGHTS AND RESPONSIBILITIES

Every family has its own rules and it doesn't matter exactly what they are so long as they are clear and consistent. There have to be sanctions and rewards, and these should be applied equally to all the children in the family.

> Having clear rules doesn't only help children to feel confident they know how to behave – it also helps parents. If you and your partner have agreed strategies for dealing with rudeness, for example, knowing exactly where you want to draw the line, and if you have discussed what sanctions you're going to use, then you won't run the risk of inadvertently undermining each other's authority. It may be necessary to compromise on some things, but that's worth doing because family rules work best when both parents stand solidly together.

Rules and sanctions need to be frequently reviewed as children grow older because from time to time things that have been effective will stop working so well or no longer feel appropriate. For example, the 'naughty step' or time-out approach can be great for young children but a stroppy teenager might be delighted to be sent to her room.

Sanctions don't need to be draconian – they just need to be a clear, quick message that you don't approve of what your child has done and that you are not prepared to let it go unremarked. Grounding your child for a month, for example, won't be more effective than for a few days, even though it might give you greater satisfaction to threaten it.

Which brings me to another point – if you've already got a menu of agreed sanctions you won't be so tempted to threaten a massive punishment on the spur of the moment that you then can't carry out because it's simply impractical. Doling out sanctions and not following through won't encourage your children to respect either you or your family rules.

Learning how to live by the rules within the family will help your child to fit in comfortably with the rules of every social group she belongs to. As well as being a member of your family, she is part of her school community and also possibly of several clubs and organizations outside school, such as Brownies or Guides. She is part of a neighbourhood which has local by-laws and a country which has laws.

You might think that some rules and laws are silly or unnecessary, but it's in your child's best interests that you encourage a healthy respect for them because they provide a solid structure within which everyone knows where they stand. If you cherry-pick, letting your child feel it's OK to obey some rules and ignore others, then you undermine the very structures that make every individual more strong.

So make sure your child is aware of rules and laws. Discourage her from breaking them and try to avoid speaking disrespectfully about teaching staff and police, whose job it is to uphold them.

Help your child understand that rules and laws don't just restrict her freedom – they give her rights. For example, the no-running-in-the-corridor rule at school restricts her freedom to run but also gives her the right not to be trampled on; outside school, the law against harassment means she can't bombard people with abusive text messages and emails but it also gives her the right not to be bombarded with them herself. Appreciating her rights will help her to accept her responsibilities and understand we are all equal under the law.

This idea of equal rights is the key to respecting both oneself and others. People who put the rights and needs of others before their own are called passive, and passive people leave themselves open to becoming victims. Aggressive people, who put their own rights and needs first, can, if unchecked, become bullies. Assertive people respect other people's rights as equal to their own. Another word for self-esteem is self-respect.

> Children can become passive or aggressive if they are not sure of their rights and responsibilities, and that's why strong rules and laws that everyone sticks to are important, but there are other factors to think about as well. Anything that undermines children's rights can make them become passive and lack the confidence to stick up for themselves. Sometimes a family which is not harmonious will present itself as a happy family because each member has given up the right to tell it like it is.

Children can easily feel obliged to give up their rights if their parents are ill, unhappy or overworked, or if their siblings are very young, very numerous or very demanding. Anything, in fact, that makes a child feel insecure in her parents' ability to love and care for her will damage her ability to speak up for herself. That's why all children are more vulnerable to bullying at times of family stress.

Here are two basic rights your child needs –

1. The right to be treated with respect
   No child should be physically, mentally or emotionally abused or humiliated. Sarcasm and swearing are examples of showing disrespect. Try not to talk to your child in ways you would not want her to talk to you. But remember that you are entitled to be treated with respect as well.
2. The right to be heard – but not the right to be right
   Every child should have her opinions taken seriously and her feelings validated without fear of being judged, belittled or ignored. But this does not mean she should necessarily have what she wants. Respecting the rights of your child does not mean giving up your own power.

Rules, rights and responsibilities are a matter of collective choice, but they provide a framework in which the individual can flourish. Values, on the other hand, are not dictated by law. We make up our own mind about ethical choices, and personal values are a vital part of our sense of self.

VALUES

Small children don't question their family's values, but as they gain experience in the world and become aware that other people have different beliefs and opinions it is natural for them to start to challenge the way their parents look at things. This is an opportunity for growth, not just for the child, but for the whole family.

Supposing your child decides it's wrong to eat meat. You

could override her feelings and coerce her into eating meat by making it very hard for her to refuse, or you could support her and even treat her new vegetarianism as an opportunity to learn some new recipes and create a more varied family diet. She may be able to persuade other family members to become vegetarian, or she may continue to be the only one, but either way your family grows and develops through being challenged.

Supposing your child becomes interested in green issues, she might feel that your family should recycle more. Again, you could block her by making it difficult, or you could support her in doing her bit for the environment by, say, putting newspapers aside for her to bag up for collection instead of just throwing them in with the old teabags and pan-scrapings. If, on consideration, you agree with her green stance you could take it further by bagging things up and doing the whole thing yourself.

But supposing your child decides your family views about neighbourliness are old-fashioned and irrelevant, and she thinks it's just hard luck if the old man next door doesn't like rock music? Let her argue her case, even though in the end you will need to put your foot down – her developing values should not stop you from living according to your own. It will be easier to draw the line at the things that really matter to you if you can manage to be flexible about the rest.

You can help your child to develop her ethical choices through conversations and discussions. If you have just seen a TV programme about graffiti, for example, you could ask, 'Do you think people should be allowed to paint on walls in public places?' and 'Why do you think some people object to it?'

instead of just grunting something about the state of the world today. If your child comes home from school with a story about someone getting sent home for dyeing their hair you could ask her whether she thinks that was fair, and talk about other dress-code rules at the school instead of just saying something dismissive like 'Serves him right'.

Children go out into the world and then bring the world back in, and if you can welcome new ideas and be open to discussion, to persuasion even, then you will help your child to explore how she feels about what's right and wrong and reach her own conclusions. Very often, your child will come down in favour of your values anyway, but she has to test them for herself in order to make them her own.

No one can have the courage of their convictions unless they know what their convictions are, and your child will be able to stand up for herself much better if she has a strong sense of who she is.

KINDNESS AND CONTRIBUTION

Your child's view of herself will be affected by the way other people see her. If she is noisy and loutish, other people will not like being around her, whereas if she is polite and considerate she will meet with approval, and that will help her to approve of herself. Generally speaking, being nice is always a good idea because then you live in a world that is well disposed towards you.

Your approval is very important to your child, even if at times she may behave as if she couldn't care less, but she also needs to gain the approval of other adults who aren't so obviously biased. Older mentors for your child could include her teacher or swimming coach, a relative or family friend. Sometimes, a best friend's parent can become a good mentor too.

Having older people she looks up to will teach your child the value of good manners, co-operation and other mature social skills that may be sketchy among her peers. If she can also find ways of making an active contribution, so much the better, because then other people will be grateful to her and being appreciated is a wonderful boost for anyone's self-esteem.

There are lots of ways your child can make a contribution. At home, she can do her share of household tasks like tidying up and mowing the lawn. Some families have a rota, or you may prefer to let your children choose an area of the housework that they will take sole responsibility for, such as putting out the rubbish or keeping the hallway tidy.

Sharing chores is obviously sensible because what takes four people half an hour each would be two solid hours for one, but don't think of it as making your own life easier – think of it as giving your children an opportunity to play an active part in the work of family life, to be useful, and to feel useful. Avoid criticizing the work they do, say thank you and remember to give praise when they've done a great job.

Outside the home, encourage your child to do some kind of voluntary work if she gets the chance or there's something she's particularly interested in. Maybe she would like to join in with a conservation project or local fundraiser, or give a few hours a week helping out at a retirement home or holiday play-scheme.

Small contributions are just as good if your child doesn't want to make a regular commitment of time. She could donate her old magazines to the local health centre and take the toys and clothes she doesn't want any more to charity shops, for example. Anything that involves thinking of other people will help her to feel good about herself.

When a child is bullied, being rejected by her social group can be a devastating blow to her self-esteem. We are social animals and how we fit into our communities is crucial to the way that we feel about ourselves.

Being part of strong, supportive social networks outside school will help to protect your child from feeling like a misfit if her friends have turned against her, and keep affirming for her that she is still a valuable and valued member of society.

Establishing good boundaries at home will enable her to develop a strong sense of herself as a separate person within a social setting. Firm family rules will give her the certainty that comes from knowing how to behave as well as providing a safe structure in which she can learn that she has exactly the same rights and responsibilities as everyone else.

Supporting your child as she develops her own values will help her to establish her identity and let her know that it's all right to be the person she wants to be.

Encouraging her to join in, be nice and make a contribution to society will give her the experience of earning other people's appreciation and respect.

This is the solid groundwork you can do to help your child experience herself as a competent and valued member of society, which is an essential aspect of good self-esteem.

While you are working in this way, notice your own feelings about how you relate to other people. Check your own boundaries and attitudes when it comes to rules and regulations. It's no good telling your child one thing and showing her another – as Jung said, children learn from what the adult is, not from what he says. So if you are not a great respecter of social structures you might want to examine your assumptions in the light of this experience and notice how rules and regulations offer protection for everybody.

This will be easy to see when your child is bullied and you want the school or the police or the bullies' parents – anyone with any authority at all – to lay down the law and stop the bullying.

RECAP POINTS

- An often-overlooked aspect of self-esteem is how we relate to other people
- Your child can get a strong sense of herself as an individual if you have firm boundaries at home
- Having respect for rules, rights and responsibilities can make your child feel safe and strong

- Allowing your child to develop her own social values will give her a sense of identity
- Encouraging her to be pleasant and make a contribution means other people will appreciate her, which will help her feel good about herself

CHAPTER SEVEN

Encouraging Self-acceptance

ChildLine did some research a few years ago in which they asked children who admitted to bullying what made them do it. Some said it was an outlet for their anger and frustration, some said they thought it was a laugh and some said they did it out of boredom – not one of them mentioned their victims' characteristics.

Yet children who are bullied usually take it personally and jump straight to the conclusion that there must be something wrong with them. They will start to examine themselves for faults and failings that might explain why anyone would hate them so much; they can easily begin to hate themselves.

Children who are bullied by someone they've thought of as a friend are particularly vulnerable to self-doubt, because if a person who knows them well and claims to like them starts using verbal abuse or personal insults, then surely they must deserve it. If the bullying spreads so that lots of people are joining in, or if it goes on for a long time, this too can seem like overwhelming evidence to the bullied child that there must be something wrong with him.

Most children can have their self-belief undermined by bullying, but some will be more affected by it than others, or will crumble more quickly. It partly depends on temperament, partly on upbringing and partly on extra stresses, such as parents splitting up.

When your child is bullied your own self-belief can also come under pressure. Your faith in yourself as a parent can falter, as you start thinking that maybe you should have done something to stop your child becoming a target and maybe you should have given him better skills for standing up for himself. You can feel a failure if you don't know what to do to rescue him.

How well your self-belief stands up to the specific situation of having a bullied child will depend partly upon how strong it is in the rest of your life. In this, as in all other areas, your child will learn from what you are, rather than what you say. He won't learn to like himself because you like him; he'll learn to like himself because you like yourself.

To find out what kind of role model you are in the area of self-acceptance, try this experiment: Stand in front of a full-length mirror and take a good long look at yourself. Turn around to see your body from different angles. Look closely at your face. Examine your hair, your skin, your mouth, nose and forehead. Take your time.

Look into your own eyes. What sort of person do you think you are? Think about the things you've done and the things you hope to do one day. Notice what you say to yourself inside your head. Stop and tell yourself out loud, 'Right now, I love myself just as I am.'

If you found it difficult to look at yourself so closely, or if you were surprised how critical you felt, or if it was hard to say 'I love myself', you're normal. Low self-esteem is a feature of our times.

One of the problems is that we live in a society where everyone is under intense pressure to be perfect.

THE PRESSURE TO BE PERFECT

Advertising has always peddled the idea that we can have the perfect family if we eat the right brand of gravy, the perfect hair if we use the right shampoo, the perfect skin if we buy the right moisturizer, but these days what's between the ads, on TV and in magazines, reinforces the same idea.

We're bombarded with lifestyle programmes and articles purporting to show us how to look better, have better living spaces, be better wives, husbands, parents – and these start from the assumption that the way we are right now somehow isn't good enough. Pampered celebrities are presented as the image of perfect youth, perfect aging, perfect wealth, perfect marriage – until, inevitably, they fall off the pedestal, to be replaced by new media darlings.

Politically, we live in a targets culture, where often unrealistic, abstract notions of what should be possible stretch workers and systems to breaking point because what 'should be' possible actually isn't.

At school, all children, whatever their natural aptitudes and learning styles, are expected to succeed in batteries of assessment tests that measure only a very narrow range of abilities. And they aren't just expected to do well – they're expected to do better year on year than children have ever done before.

Nothing is ever good enough because there's always a new ideal to aim for, and while it's a good thing to have aspirations, if they aren't attainable they can leave people feeling helpless and inadequate. Most of us these days think there's something wrong with us, but the only thing that's wrong is that we're chasing unrealistic goals.

Setting ourselves unrealistic standards and not feeling good enough is a double-whammy to our self-esteem – first, it makes us unhappy with the way we are and, second, it actually stops us reaching our full potential.

Take looks, for example. How many women do you know who are perfectly happy with their appearance? Almost everyone I know has some sort of beauty worry. People who feel fat hide themselves under lots of layers or squeeze into tight undergarments which make them look self-conscious and uncomfortable.

People who feel they have poor skin, crooked teeth, a big

nose or bags under their eyes will limit their facial expressions and look away when they're talking to you. In so many subtle ways we actually draw attention to our imperfections by trying to disguise them, and so we make ourselves less attractive. A woman who is happy in her own skin will look good even if she doesn't conform to conventional notions of beauty.

In the family context, wanting to be a perfect parent is going to give you a lot of anxiety and put pressure on your child, and this will show in your relationship. No one can get it right all the time, so accepting that you are a good-and-bad parent means no one has to worry about it. Accepting you have a normal, good-and-bad child means you'll never have to be disappointed.

For good self-esteem, instead of trying to be perfect, try to be yourself – your whole self, warts and all. Because, when it comes to being yourself, you're the expert. Have another go at the mirror experiment, telling yourself all the things you usually do – 'My legs are too fat . . . my face is too narrow . . . my mouth turns down at the corners . . . I'm a worrier . . . I haven't really done anything with my life . . .' Then let go of the need to be perfect. So you've got fat legs, a thin face, a grumpy mouth and a tendency to fret. So you never made it to prime minister. So what?

When you stop fighting the bad stuff, you're much more able to notice the good. 'I *have* got expressive eyes . . . straight shoulders . . . a nice neck . . . I *am* quite caring . . . I am bringing up two children and doing a job I like . . .'

You can say, 'Right now, I look wonderful' because you do – you look wonderfully yourself. You can say 'I love myself' because you are not laying down conditions, and that's what love is.

ACCEPTING IMPERFECTIONS

Accepting your imperfections is brilliant protection from bullying because it means you don't have to worry about criticism. If someone taunts you for being hopeless at sports and you know you are, then you don't have to get defensive – if you not only know it but fully accept it, because nobody's perfect, then you'll find it much easier to let their rudeness go. As soon as not being sporty stops being a problem to you, then anyone who taunts you for it becomes the one with the problem.

What bullies look for in a victim isn't someone who has actually got something wrong with them – it's someone who has got something that worries them, something they feel insecure about. This may be to do with three things: appearance, personality, or faults and failings.

Appearance

You may be perfectly happy with your own appearance in a looks-don't-matter kind of way, but it's worth remembering that for your child looks almost certainly will matter, simply because of the age and stage he's at. Young people can feel extremely sensitive about their appearance and telling them they look fine and just shouldn't worry about it might not feel very supportive.

While you wouldn't want to bankrupt yourself getting the

latest designer clothes for him, let him choose his own things within your budget and give him positive feedback on his choices.

If he tells you something is bothering him about his appearance, don't dismiss it out of hand. Help him to change it if he can, as in the case of crooked teeth, and to accept it if he can't, for example if he's a foot taller than the rest of his class.

Point out that nobody looks perfect – even models are digitally enhanced and need a troop of stylists following them around 24/7. Get him to notice how having friends and even falling in love can happen to everyone, no matter what they look like, and in the end that is the most important thing.

Personality

When someone criticizes your character it strikes to the very heart of your being. Children who aren't very sociable – creative, studious or quiet types – can become a target for teasing. Trying to make such a child be more outgoing and interested in group activities would be to reinforce the notion that there's something wrong with the way he is.

> Sociable children who long to be part of a group can become the patsy, or be forever falling out with their friendship group. It might feel like a good idea to try to protect such a child from pain by telling him he doesn't need to have lots of friends and he's fine on his own –

> but that would also be to make him feel he isn't all right the way he is. The best thing you can do for your child is to affirm and acknowledge him by allowing him to explore his own temperament outside the pressure of school life. If he's quiet and creative, let him spend all day on Photoshop – let him enjoy doing what comes naturally to him.

If he's sociable but finds it hard to make good relationships, think about where he might be going wrong. Maybe he gets on well in one-to-one situations but finds groups difficult, so is he trying to dominate the group? Is he rushing in to new groups without first holding back a little to get the lie of the land and understand how the group works? Help him to enjoy the social skills he's got by letting him have friends over, even if sometimes it all goes wrong, and then talk things over with him and see if you can suggest a strategy for avoiding the same problem in the future.

You can't help your child to withstand attacks on his personality by joining in and trying to make him be different. That will only make him weaker. Help him to feel strong and secure in himself by accepting him exactly as he is. He doesn't need to change, he needs to develop; so try to give him plenty of opportunities and encouragement to make the best of who he is instead of trying to make him want to be someone he isn't.

Faults and Failings

It's easier to accept your faults and failings if you can adopt a positive attitude towards them. Just as you can choose to look upon problems and setbacks as learning opportunities, so you can see your faults and failings as part of the natural process of living and growing.

To err is human and yet we can all find it hard to admit when we've made a mistake. That's a pity because if you can't admit your mistakes you can't learn from them, and also you'll be more put out if someone else takes you up on them.

Supposing you said something nasty to a friend and they turned round and told you they thought you were out of order. You could go on the defensive and say it was just a joke, or that you only said it because it was true. You could go on the attack by telling them they've got no sense of humour or shouldn't be so annoying in the first place. Or you could admit that, on consideration, maybe you were out of order, and you're sorry.

Admitting you've made a mistake feels bad, but that's the point about it – because you don't want to feel that way again, you don't make the same mistake again. Next time your friend annoys you maybe you'll stop short of the sarcastic put-down, and in this way you'll be developing kindness and consideration in yourself.

When your child makes a mistake, even if it's quite a serious one such as taking something that doesn't belong to him, you can help him deal with it in a positive way by acknowledging his courage in owning up, making sure he understands the consequences of that behaviour – upset feelings, loss of trust – and giving an appropriate punishment. You can ask him to apologize and, if possible, try to make amends.

Then let it go – this is the really important bit. Your child will feel less anxious about making mistakes and more willing to own up to them if he knows that you won't make a major issue out of everything or keep reminding him of things he's done wrong.

The other thing to be very clear about is that your child is bigger than his mistakes, so take care that you focus on the behaviour rather than the person. You might tell him he has behaved selfishly, but that doesn't make him a selfish person. Such labels can be very hard to shift.

Encouraging your child to see mistakes as a natural way of growing throughout life will make it much easier for him to take them in his stride. Say some other children have a go at him for making their teacher keep the whole class in because he was being silly, then he will be able to admit it and promise not to do it again rather than argue, blame everyone else or become overwhelmed by shame – any of which might make the others turn against him even more.

BUILDING STRENGTHS

Accepting that you aren't perfect is one side of the coin when it comes to feeling happy with yourself – the other side is recognizing and building upon your strengths.

Even though it can sometimes be difficult to see them, everyone has plenty of real strengths, both in the area of skills and knowledge and in terms of personal qualities.

Skills and Knowledge

Skills and knowledge come out of your everyday experience but you might not even notice them for various reasons.

- Once you've mastered something, you do it without thinking about it

  For example, supposing you've got a dog, you and your child will know lots of things that non-dog-owners don't know, such as how often they need feeding, how much exercise they need and how to stop them leaving little heaps on the carpet.

- Most people think competitively

  Because we always want to be 'good' or 'the best' we can underestimate our real achievements. For example, reading and writing is a fantastic skill that most people have but many discount or undervalue because they didn't get great grades in school.

  People who play for a local sports team may think they're not very good because they aren't in a national team, even though they must be streets ahead of most other players.

- The things you're best at aren't always the ones that are most highly valued within your family or at school

  Say you loved drawing when you were younger but your family thought art was a waste of time? Or supposing you were brilliant at making friends at school but all you ever got tested on was academic work? Then you might realize that you had ability but you might not recognize how much it was worth.

Most children have an astonishing knowledge of things they're interested in, such as complete recall of every player in the Premiership or all the steps in pop dance routines or the history of the dinosaurs or the first five series of *The Simpsons.*

You can help your child to become aware of all the things he knows by showing an interest and letting him share his enthusiasm with you. You can help him extend his knowledge and skills by, for example, taking him to a Premiership match or a dinosaur museum, or buying him a dance mat or a *Simpsons* video game.

It doesn't matter what fires your child's interest – anything he's keen on will provide him with a learning experience that is easy and rewarding, because the ability to learn is directly linked to how interested we are in the subject. A child who is bored and underachieving at school because he doesn't see the point in knowing how rivers are formed or what happened in the run-up to the Second World War can still experience himself as a vibrant and capable learner if he finds a hobby or interest that really engages him.

This is the crucial thing – it has to be your child's own choice, not yours. So if your child expresses an interest in, say, tae kwon do, however pointless and unappealing it may seem to you, encourage him to have a go. Hobbies and interests are one area where we can all achieve satisfaction and success, and the experience of success is very good for a person's self-esteem.

It may be worth bearing in mind as well, when you're driving your child to his drama workshop or brass band practice, that a hobby can flag up special aptitudes that could later develop into a satisfying career or at the very least give him confidence and skills that he can take forward into his next learning adventure.

Personal Qualities

Good personal qualities like patience and kindness are part of human nature and that means everyone's got them. But we don't often recognize them in ourselves because:

- We regard goodness as a given
  In an ideal world where everything was how it should be, being good would be nothing special, but in the real world, it's a choice. People can choose to be mean, lazy, aggressive, impatient, rude – so if you don't act like that, you have made a positive choice you can feel good about.
- We think we should be good 24/7
  We don't give ourselves credit for the times we show kindness or patience – we just beat ourselves up about the times we don't. We might feel a sense of failure for snapping at an irritating colleague, for example, but not recognize the triumph of self-control that means we manage not to snap very often.

- We don't want to get too full of ourselves
  Modesty is an admirable quality but I want to put in a good word at this point for pride. Expressions such as 'Pride comes before a fall' give pride a bad press, but it's actually a good and proper response to personal achievement.
- Being proud of yourself when you get things right doesn't mean you're in danger of getting too full of yourself, for the simple reason that you won't get things right all the time.
- Being proud of your child doesn't mean you're taking credit for his achievements – it means you're enjoying and acknowledging them.

Simply becoming aware of your good qualities can help you to develop them as they become part of your identity. To see whether you identify more with your faults or fine qualities, think about how you respond to criticism and compliments. Which do you take most notice of? Which do you believe?

If you seem to be more aware of your faults than your positive qualities, take more notice when people say nice things about you – treat compliments as useful information.

You could also try the 'two sides test'. Write a list of all the things you don't like about yourself, such as 'I'm bossy' or 'I'm oversensitive' – make it as long as you like. Then think about how you might regard those 'weaknesses' as a side of your strengths – 'I'm a good leader' or 'I'm quite caring'.

This is an interesting thing to do when you're thinking about your child as well – write down his weaknesses and let them reveal the potential strengths that you could consciously nurture in him.

The 'two sides test' also works the other way round – a list of your strengths can also reveal potential weaknesses. Another variation is to think of five positive qualities you like about yourself and five negative ones and then see if some of them match up as different sides of the same coin.

You can do the 'two sides test' on anyone you know to help you adopt a balanced view. No one is all good or all bad, and seeing both sides can mean that all your relationships become more comfortable and more real, particularly your relationship with yourself.

BEING YOUR OWN BEST FRIEND

Your relationship with yourself is the most important relationship in your life. As well as being the only one that will definitely last until the day you die, it sets the tone for all your relationships with other people. It is also the model on which your child will form his own relationship with himself. Getting that right is the most important thing for him if he's being bullied, even more important than trying to find new friends. It may actually be a necessary first step.

At times of stress, any cracks in a relationship begin to show. A child who has always seemed happy in his own skin can become brutally self-critical and self-rejecting if he is subjected to a prolonged period of bullying. So can a parent who has to stand helplessly by.

If you are giving yourself a hard time for not knowing how to handle the situation, if you are feeling stupid or inadequate or guilty, imagine you were your own best friend. Would you still be saying, 'Sending him to school was a stupid thing to do' and 'It's your fault he's so upset'? Or, to take the other scenario, 'Not sending him to school was a stupid thing to do. It's all your fault he's school-phobic.'

> Give yourself the help and support you would give your best friend. Don't beat yourself up if you don't know what to do, and you sometimes get it wrong. Show your child that it's all right to have problems, to try to solve them, to make mistakes and to move on.

If your child is being bullied you'll probably have lots of opportunities to wonder whether you are doing the right thing. Should you insist on him doing PE? Should you give him a note? Should you make him go on the school bus? Should you talk to his teacher? There will doubtless be occasions when you think you've made a mistake. Here is a useful technique for giving yourself support at times when you feel beset by self-doubt or self-criticism.

Write a letter, imagining it is to a close friend. Tell them everything that's been going on, what you've done and how you feel about it. Really pour your heart out, and don't worry at all about getting your grammar right or anything like that.

Then read your letter, imagining it's *from* a close friend, and write a reply. This letter will be full of all the encouragement, advice and support you need to help you weather the storm, and it will be an effective antidote to all the harsh things you might otherwise be saying to yourself.

Another thing you can do when your self-esteem takes a dip is to get active. Distract yourself as you might try to distract a friend, by doing something nurturing and pleasurable. This might include spending time with your real-life friends, who can easily get shut out at times when you aren't getting on well with yourself.

When it comes to self-acceptance, perfectionism is the enemy. It's no good knocking yourself out trying to be perfect or sinking into helpless despondency when you fail. Accepting that you aren't perfect means you don't have to worry so much about criticism and you are able to work on your imperfections.

Noticing and valuing all the great skills and qualities you've got going for you makes it much easier to feel good about yourself, and that's what self-esteem is.

Being a good friend to yourself means you will be providing the best possible role model for your child and showing him that bullying, like every other setback, doesn't have to fill you with feelings of failure and self-dislike. Everything is survivable as long as you don't reject and abandon yourself.

RECAP POINTS

- Anyone can be undermined by bullying, falling prey to feelings of self-doubt and self-dislike
- Perfectionism makes people more vulnerable
- Self-esteem is about accepting your imperfections and building upon your strengths
- Having good self-esteem will enable your child to be a loyal friend to himself, which is particularly important if he is being bullied

Chapter Eight

Nurturing Self-confidence

A child who is being bullied can develop a terrifying fear – the fear of being herself. She can lose her spontaneity, always trying to spot and weed out any aspect of her normal behaviour that might trigger taunts and teasing, and attempting to imitate other people who don't seem to be such a target.

A gulf can grow up between her authentic self and the way she expresses herself in the world, and then she can feel confused, lost, not even sure any more who she really is. As her sense of herself slips away, she may start to depend on other people to tell her what she should think and feel, and how she should act. She may feel vulnerable, need lots of reassurance and dislike change, wanting to control her environment to protect herself from unexpected developments.

You can help your child hold on to her sense of self by encouraging her to explore and express her emotions and the world of her imagination, and to keep sight of her dreams.

Emotions and imagination are the foundations of self

because they are unique to the individual; they cannot be shared or acquired like practical skills and intellectual knowledge. Hopes and dreams provide a sense of direction, and the energy to become the most that you can be.

EXPRESSING EMOTIONS

Acknowledging your child's and your own emotions is important if the child is to learn to trust her emotions, and therefore to trust herself. If you deny your own feelings, what the child senses will be at odds with what she is told and she will become mystified and confused. If you deny her feelings, you are encouraging her to deny them too, and any loss of authentic emotion is always a loss of self.

It can be tempting, especially when someone is trying to express painful feelings, to bribe or cajole her out of them, and almost all of us at times use humour and irony to protect ourselves from painful emotions.

If you talk about your feelings openly and without embarrassment, you will be showing your child it's safe for her to do so as well. You will also be giving her a language for expressing the full range of her own emotions.

This isn't to say, of course, that you should turn your domestic life into some sort of melodrama. It isn't a question of *having* more emotion, but of *expressing* more emotion. So, if you've just had a visit from a favourite neighbour, instead of saying, 'That was nice', you might say, 'I really love it when he calls in' or 'I do enjoy his company'.

If someone's said something horrible to you, instead of crashing plates in the kitchen and refusing to talk about it, you could say that you're feeling upset, hurt, angry or alarmed. Putting into words exactly how you feel is the best way for you to work through your feelings, and it makes other people feel safer because they know what's going on and can respond appropriately.

Besides setting an example in this way, you can encourage your child to express her emotions by simply reading her body language and hazarding a guess. If she's lazing around on the settee, instead of saying, 'Haven't you got anything to do?' you could ask her, 'Are you feeling bored?' (or fed up, lonely, ill, unsociable, if that's the way she looks).

> Quite often, bullied children do manage to tell someone what's happening, but can't bring themselves to talk about how they feel. This leaves them trying to cope with some very intense emotions on their own. Helping your child talk about her less difficult feelings will make it much easier for her to share her most frightening ones.

Young children who find it difficult to talk about their feelings will often express them in play. You can use a favourite doll or cuddly toy as your mouthpiece – 'Big Bear's worried about you today; he thinks you look sad' – and let your child talk to you through him. Or you can use the toy as a mouthpiece for your child – 'Is Big Bear sad today? What's upset you, Big Bear?'

If your child is too old to talk to her toys, she might prefer to talk to an animal. Children of all ages and, indeed, many adults find they can talk to their pets about their most profound feelings. Even looking after a small animal like a rat or a hamster can teach your child a lot about herself, as well as giving her the experience of being responsible and nurturing.

Besides talking about emotions you could encourage your child to explore and express them in other ways. Writing, for example, is more private and so it might feel like a safer place to start than talking to someone else; it can also help your child understand what she's feeling and so be able to talk about it more easily.

You could suggest to your child that she keeps a diary to record events and, in particular, the way she feels about them. Writing is a good way of objectifying experience because when you put your feelings down on the page, you are separating yourself from them. That's why so many people come to terms with extreme suffering by writing a book about it.

Perhaps you could buy her a beautiful hardback note-book, or get her to choose one for herself – a plain notebook will be better than a printed diary because then she need not feel restricted on days when she's got a lot to say, or obliged to write something on days when she doesn't feel like it.

Suggest that she treats her diary like a trusted friend who will keep all her secrets, because no one else will ever read what she has written in it unless she wants them to. Tell her to keep it at home in a secret place where none of her schoolmates might stumble upon it. Give her some lovely coloured gel pens and a glue stick so she can add pictures if she wants to, because this will help her value and cherish her writing, which is a way of valuing and cherishing herself.

Another idea for getting your child to express her feelings about the bullying situation is to suggest she write letters to everyone involved – the people bullying her, of course, but also perhaps some of her teachers and friends, whom she might feel grateful to for sticking up for her, or angry with for not helping.

The idea of these letters is to release pent-up emotions and gain clarity, and a crucial aspect of this is that they are defi-nitely *not* intended for sending. Knowing she will not send them is what will give her the freedom to express exactly what she's feeling without censoring anything. They will probably be great pieces of writing because they'll be fuelled by passion, and she may want to stick them in her diary and keep them.

If your child would like to actually send a letter or email about her situation then there are lots of reputable websites and helplines she could contact – some addresses are in the back of this book. She could also use chatrooms and message boards for letting off steam, but you will want to be sure she knows how to use these things sensibly and safely. So long as she understands that the people she meets online might not be who they say they are and that she should never give any personal details about herself or agree to meet anyone without your permission, it can be good for her to have some virtual friends when her real friends aren't being supportive.

If your child is more visual than verbal she might prefer to keep a picture diary. When she feels like recording her day, she can draw a picture-strip or cartoon of what happened and add a few words. Or she can make a drawing of herself, adding things that express how she was feeling. She might be indoors, in a dark room, or outside in a sunny meadow. There might be wolves around her or kittens. She might be on her own or among friends.

When she does this, your child will naturally choose colours and images that express her emotions, and building a picture will be a way for her to literally see how she feels.

Music is another great way of expressing emotions, either through listening or playing. Your child might want to listen to lots of angry, thumping music, or sad soulful songs – if it drives you mad, you could get her some headphones rather than issuing a ban.

You can use any of these techniques yourself in order to gain some mastery over the strong emotions you will be feeling if your child is being bullied, and you might be surprised at how powerful they can be. Take your time, work from the heart and don't worry about it being 'good'. If you haven't done much writing or drawing since you were at school, you might be surprised how naturally it can come when you're doing it for yourself and you know no one will be judging it.

Your child needs to know that all her emotions are natural and normal, even though, especially during adolescence, they could feel very extreme. She can think of emotions like the weather, with everyone having some days that are just naturally more sunny or dull than others, and suffering occasional storms and depressions.

She can explore her own emotional climate, noticing if she is normally cool and calm, or moody and changeable, or bubbly and bright.

She can experience her emotions in a safe way through talking and using creative activities, and that will help her not to act them out or numb them down, either of which could be very damaging to her confidence in herself.

EXPRESSING IMAGINATION

Imagine your ideal garden. Close your eyes and really picture it. Walk around it, noticing the plants, the paths, the walls, hedges or fences, and any seating areas, water features or sculptures. Take a few moments for this before you read on.

Now imagine that you could invent a brand new breed of dog. Picture it in your mind's eye. How big is it? What sort of fur has it got? What shape is its body and head? Make it as fanciful as you like – mine has green tiger stripes and orange eyes.

Now imagine that the postman has brought you a parcel. Pick it up and examine it. How heavy is it? How many stamps does it have? Is it sealed with Sellotape or string? Start to open it . . . what's inside?

If I were to ask ten thousand people to do those three little exercises, every one of them would imagine something different – no two images would be exactly the same. That's the incredible thing about the imagination – it creates images that are completely unique to every person.

What if I were to ask you to write about your imagined garden, dog and parcel, or draw a picture of them? You might balk at that and say you're no good at making things up – but all I'd be asking you to do is describe something you've already seen in your mind's eye. It's very simple, and yet an amazing number of people feel they have 'no imagination' or 'aren't creative'.

Creative writing and drawing is something most of us don't do unless we either feel we're good at it or are getting paid for it, or preferably both, That seems a shame because every young child has the urge, the ability and the confidence to create visual images, and in other cultures this is nurtured and valued into adult life.

Expressing yourself creatively means exploring your own inner world, the world of your imagination, noticing your uniqueness and experiencing complete control, because in that world you are the one making the rules. Creating something also means taking an active role rather than passively accepting what life brings, and for all these reasons creative self-expression can be fantastically empowering for any child who is being bullied. But that isn't all.

As well as being enjoyable and affirming, making stories and drawings can also be a way of working towards solutions for problems in the outer world, because whatever you dream up is coming from your unconscious mind and will have a symbolic relationship with your current preoccupations and concerns. Although you may not be aware of any link at all between the products of your imagination and your real life, it will be there.

In stories, you will be working out your problems in the lives of your heroes and villains. For example, years ago, when I was asked to write a myth or legend, the first one I thought of was Androcles and the lion. At that time, I was just starting to be published, and I was feeling unnerved and vulnerable about having parts of my inner world exposed to other people's scrutiny. This seems to happen to a lot of writers when they first get published.

Androcles

Androcles was a Roman slave who escaped on a trading trip to Africa. On the run, he came across a huge lion with a thorn in its paw and, although he was absolutely petrified, he took pity on the beast and pulled the thorn out.

Androcles and the lion lived together in a cave for several years until Androcles started to pine for his family and friends in Rome. He thought no one would recognize him if he went back – but they did. He was put in chains and taken to the arena.

Runaway slaves were fed to the lions and – you guessed it – the lion that Androcles eventually found himself face to face with in the arena was the very same one he had helped. The crowd was so amazed to see a hungry lion lie down in front of a slave that the emperor pardoned Androcles and gave him the lion as a present.

Shortly after I wrote it, I realized that Androcles' story resonated with me at that moment because I needed to find courage in myself to meet the new challenge of being a published writer. You only notice the relevance of your stories to whatever is going on in your life after they are written, and sometimes not until years later – it's completely unconscious.

A retelling can be an easy way to start if you fancy having a go at story-writing. Think of the first myth, legend or fairy tale that comes into your head. Write it down, not worrying too much if you can't remember all the details – the parts you remember will be the ones that matter in this context. Don't worry in the slightest about trying to make it 'good'.

When you have finished, consider the main characters – what are they like and what challenges are they facing? Stories always involve problems and setbacks, and heroes always have to find inner resources in order to deal with them. See if any parallels with your own situation jump out at you, but if not, keep the story in the back of your mind and the reasons you chose it will gradually become apparent.

The stories you like reading will also reflect the big issues and concerns in your life, so think about the books you remember best, the stories that have touched you most. Encourage your child to read stories as well, so that she can have the experience of being a hero and finding the resourcefulness to face up to problems and setbacks. Imaginary experience works in exactly the same way as real-life experience in deepening your understanding of yourself and life.

Creative artwork, like writing, will also have symbolic relevance to your current situation, although it may be even harder to see. If you choose to draw lightning flashes or daggers or raging lions they might be expressions of anger; if you draw a beautiful room maybe what you want right now is somewhere to retreat to, a place of safety.

If painting feels like a step too far you could try collage. All you need is a pile of old magazines, a piece of paper and a glue stick. Start by giving yourself five minutes to tear out any images, patterns, words or colours that appeal to you – don't be choosy, just go with your instinct.

Then cut or tear the images to fit on the paper in any way you like – maybe separate, maybe overlapping, maybe right up to the edges or only in the middle.

This process will give you the experience of feeling how colours and shapes produce an emotional reaction, and the images you have chosen will be expressive of where you are right now.

The act of creating something takes you away from the worries of everyday life and gives an experience of flow, and so it becomes a sort of meditation, making it a great solution to stress.

You can combine creative drawing with writing by using words as the focus for a picture. One of my children made a beautiful papier-mâché frame around the 'Serenity Prayer':

Grant me the serenity to accept the things I cannot change, the courage to change the things I can and the wisdom to know the difference.

Another made a picture of a sunny meadow, with the words

POSITIVE MENTAL ATTITUDE!

under a huge rainbow.

Spending time on this kind of work is a way of gaining a deeper understanding of the ideas you're trying to develop. It's also fun. It requires very little in the way of materials and no particular skill.

Having the kind of household which encourages creative self-expression doesn't mean that everyone in it is drawing and writing all the time. It's more a question of attitude. 'I'm no good at it' and 'What's the point?' are kiss-of-death attitudes when it comes to creativity. 'Everyone can do it' and 'It's a great way of understanding yourself and the world' mean you are not closing off that avenue for your child.

There are lots of other ways besides drawing and writing in which your child might enjoy expressing her creativity, for example, music, fashion, cooking or gardening. Creative self-expression will help her to enjoy being herself, understand her issues and work towards solutions; it will also help her to realize her secret dreams and fantasies about herself.

GOALS AND DREAMS

Everyone needs goals to give them a sense of direction and purpose in life, even if they don't always achieve them. Trying to live without goals would be like trying to play football without goals – yet that's what people with low self-esteem do. They don't dare to set themselves goals or try very hard because they're afraid of failing.

People with high self-esteem are afraid of failing too, but that doesn't stop them trying – it makes them even more determined to succeed. The difference is in the way they view failure, not as a catastrophe but as a step along the way. A fine example is Thomas Edison, who invented the light bulb – he famously said that he didn't regard the hundreds of experiments he tried before his eureka moment as failures but as successful attempts at finding out what didn't work.

Some people have dreams but don't think they will ever be able to achieve them, and some people don't even dare to dream. If you want your child to have the courage to go for what she wants, it might be a good idea to think about the attitudes you are modelling for her. Are you aware of having any secret ambitions? Are you doing anything about them? If not, can you think of something now that you would like to achieve? Can you work out a plan and get going?

When you are going for a long-term goal, you need to set short-term goals that will help you work towards it. For example, supposing you want to be able to play the piano. That's a long-term goal because it won't happen overnight. Your short-term goals could be to find a piano teacher, organize a regular babysitter, free up some time for practising, earn some extra money to pay for lessons, and get a piano. By breaking the goal down into incremental achievements, it becomes more easily attainable.

You wouldn't want to push your child into setting goals, but simply being aware of this approach might mean that when she expresses an interest in something you can help her work out a plan and really go for it. You can use visualization to help you feel confident that she can succeed, and your confidence will transfer itself to her. When she stumbles, you can treat her setbacks as no more than that, and help her to keep focusing forwards on what she wants to achieve.

There's a little game called 'Now, forever, never' that you might like to try if you want to uncover your child's dreams for herself, and possibly even some of your own. Get some friends or family members together and give everyone three identical strips of paper. Ask everyone to write down something they'd like to do really soon on the first piece, their lifetime dream on the second and something they'd definitely never like to do on the third. For example, mine might be: 'Now – try the new Italian restaurant in town; forever – write a bestseller; never – take up aerobics.'

Fold the pieces of paper up and put them in the middle, then take turns picking one out and trying to guess whose it is. If you guess right, you keep that piece of paper but if you guess wrong you have to refold it and put it back in the middle. The one with the most pieces of paper at the end wins.

Your child's goals may not be the goals you would want her to have. Perhaps she dreams of being a TV presenter, but you would like her to go into law. Perhaps she wants to do the lights in the school play but you think she should be up on stage. Perhaps she wants to work her way through all the *Buffy* books but you would rather she got stuck into Jane Austen. But being positive about her goals is a way of being positive about your child.

Encouraging your child to express her emotions and imagination may sometimes be challenging for you. Her painful feelings will be painful for you, and if she writes dark poems or paints violent pictures you may find that quite unsettling. Helping your child to follow her dreams for herself may also bring up some resistance in you.

But when your child is being bullied she needs to hold on to a strong sense of who she is, and not abandon herself, and that means claiming her right to feel the emotions she is feeling, to express her inner world and to pursue her personal goals and dreams. In all this, your unconditional support will be wonderfully affirming for her.

Acknowledging your own emotions, creative instincts and dreams means you will be showing her the way and it will also help you to cope in difficult circumstances. Just as your child needs to defend herself from the anger and aggression of those who are bullying her, you may need to defend yourself from your child's anger and aggression, at least until she learns to use it in constructive ways.

RECAP POINTS

- Bullying can provoke strong emotions that your child may feel unable to express
- Talking and creative activities are safe ways of experiencing emotions instead of numbing them down
- Imagination is unique to every person and expressing hers can help your child experience and enjoy her individuality
- You can encourage your child to honour her hopes and dreams by helping her set realistic goals and work towards them

CHAPTER NINE

Using Anger

Anybody who is being pushed around, teased and taunted, threatened and excluded, is bound to feel angry.

The good news is that anger is pure energy. It gives us the power to stand up for our rights, to protect our boundaries and to express our most pressing needs and desires.

We talk of anger in terms of heat – we can have a fiery temper, get hot under the collar, engage in heated discussions. Anger is the spark that ignites a burning ambition, a flaming passion. It is generated every time we are thwarted, and it spurs us on to greater effort. For a bullied child, it can be the power that turns the situation around.

The bad news is that, just like fire, anger can be dangerous and destructive if it isn't properly managed, and children who are being bullied will often experience such intense feelings of anger that their normal coping skills are completely inadequate. They can't express their anger directly to the people they are angry with so it builds up under pressure and becomes too hot to handle.

Bullied children may try to get rid of their anger in two ways. Some will deflect it by becoming unusually aggressive and taking their anger out on other people who are not connected with the bullying at all. Others will damp it down by turning it inward and becoming depressed or self-destructive. Many children will do both.

IF YOUR CHILD BEHAVES AGGRESSIVELY AT HOME

This is not at all unusual with bullied children and it might in fact be the first sign you see that makes you wonder if your child is being picked on at school.

Andrew

Thirteen-year-old Andrew had a new mobile phone for his birthday. It wasn't the exact one he wanted because that one was too expensive, but it was a lot better than his old one and he was looking forward to showing it to his friends at school.

Things started badly when one of them said something disparaging about it and soon everyone was joining in, pointing out all the phone's shortcomings and generally teasing him about it.

Andrew felt confused and flustered. He tried to hide his new phone away, but the other boys kept sending him text messages so he couldn't.

When Andrew got home he just wanted to be on his own so when his mother asked him if he'd had a good day he mumbled something and went straight to his room. He was furious with his parents for making him look an idiot, giving him a stupid phone when it would have cost only another hundred pounds or so to get him a decent one.

Andrew knew he couldn't say what he was thinking so he just crashed around in a bad mood for the rest of the week, leaving his mother completely mystified about what had got into him.

If your child behaves aggressively at home, you can react in any of four ways:

- Get angry too
  This increases the general level of anger in the family. It allows your child to alienate you and so lose his most valuable ally. It makes his anger even more frightening and difficult to control.
- Get angry and pass it on
  This is called 'kicking the cat'. Your child shouts at you for asking him to tidy his room, and that puts you in a bad mood. You snap at your younger child for some trivial misdemeanour, and that makes her angry too. So she looks around for someone to take it out on . . . Watch out, cat! 'Kicking the cat' is what Andrew did when he got angry with the boys at school and took it out on his mother.
- Feel resentful, but not say anything

This puts you in martyr mode. Your energy's all tied up with keeping your anger in, and you've none left over to help your child. Also, everyone knows the situation is volatile and you could be about to blow your top at any minute.

- Remember the game of hot potatoes . . . and give it back
  The key to giving the hot potato back is not to take things personally. Focus on the fact that the anger and bad feelings are his problem, not yours. As soon as they become your problem you are no longer in a position to help your child.

It may be hard to believe, but outbursts of aggression are usually a plea for help. The aggressive child has an urgent need for recognition and reassurance, but he also needs firm boundaries. He wants you to help him control his anger because then it will feel less dangerous.

Make it clear to your child that you are willing to listen sympathetically to what he has to say, but only if he talks to you properly, without swearing or shouting. How successful this is may depend upon how well you can manage not to swear and shout yourself.

One way of avoiding being drawn into an argument is to reply to his demands and accusations with a question. If he says, for example, 'You're always getting at me!' you might ask, 'Why do you feel I'm getting at you?' or 'Do you feel as if I'm getting at you now?' Needless to say, these questions should sound neutral and not accusing.

If your child causes problems at home by picking fights with his brothers and sisters, your best bet for defusing the situation is to offer to hear both sides of the argument one at a time, but only if nobody shouts or interrupts.

If you think it might work, you could try the no-blame approach, getting each child to look at things from the other's point of view, by asking them to express their own feelings and imagine how the other one feels. The advantage of this is that it gives your child a chance to apologize without suffering a loss of face.

For example, supposing your child has forced his younger sister off the computer without giving her a chance to finish what she was doing. If you say, 'That was really bad – how could you be so horrible to your sister?' your child would probably become defensive and protest that he wasn't being horrible, and anyway his sister deserves it because she shouldn't hog the computer all the time. Then his sister would hotly deny that she had more than her share of computer time, and so the argument would develop.

But if you were to say, 'I'm sure you didn't mean to upset your sister,' that would give your child a chance to agree and apologize – yes, he wanted to go on the computer but he didn't want to hurt anyone. This would put all three of you on the same side and you could get on with negotiating how to allocate time for each child to use the computer. You might all secretly believe that he did intend to upset his sister, but putting that on one side is simply pragmatic because it means you can defuse the situation and achieve a peaceful solution.

When your child behaves aggressively towards other family members, including you, he should always be made to apologize, whether or not he accepts that he did it deliberately – 'I didn't mean to upset you and so, if I did, I'm sorry'.

Asking for an apology sends a clear message to him that you will not allow bad behaviour to go unchallenged. It also makes him acknowledge that what he did wasn't all right. People who bully are fond of saying things like 'No hard feelings, then', 'It's all water under the bridge' and even in retrospect, 'We can laugh about it now'. They need to be told, 'Well, actually, no. Not until you apologize.'

It can be hard work standing your ground but it's important because if you let your child get out of control things will only get harder for you and more alarming for him.

Some children are naturally more aggressive than others, and some have failed to learn how to cope with anger at an earlier age. An aggressive child might have learned as a toddler that he can get what he wants by throwing a tantrum. As using anger aggressively works for him, he may not have had to discover more constructive ways of coping with it.

Fortunately, it's never too late to learn. So as much as you can, try not to give your child whatever he wants when he becomes aggressive at home – don't even give him the satisfaction of drawing you into an argument. But do give him what he needs, and that is to have his feelings recognized and acknowledged. Offering to listen to him if he talks to you properly will be a big incentive; refusing to listen if he's ranting and raving at you will be a powerful sanction,

IF YOUR CHILD BECOMES DEPRESSED OR SELF-DESTRUCTIVE

This, also, is a cry for help. But it can be as hard to see how to help a child who is withdrawn and distant as one who is hostile and full of rage.

Once again, the first thing to do is to remind yourself that it's his problem and not yours. If you become anxious and depressed as well, you won't be able to help your child. If you get frustrated and angry about having him moping around all the time, you will simply be reinforcing his own negative feelings about himself.

A passive child may be introverted and withdrawn by nature, or he may have learned to cope with angry feelings by turning them in on himself at an earlier stage. He may have been discouraged from expressing anger because his parents were ill, fragile, over-worked or perhaps afraid of expressing anger themselves. He may have been pacified, rather than satisfied. He may simply have discovered that there was no point in expressing anger because it never got him the recognition he wanted. Perhaps being depressed proved to be a more effective way of dealing with his situation, or perhaps it's the way he sees you or your partner deal with yours.

If your child is depressed, he will probably not even be aware of the anger that's at the root of his depression. He may not be experiencing anger at all, like Lewis.

Tom and Lewis

When the other boys in their class found out that Tom and Lewis had been going to weekend ballet classes they kept teasing them for being a pair of sissies.

Tom felt angry – he liked going to ballet and he wasn't going to let them spoil it for him. But Lewis felt anxious and upset. He was embarrassed about liking ballet and instead of feeling angry with the other boys for teasing him, he felt fed up with himself for being such a sissy.

Anger is the appropriate response to bullying and if a child can't feel angry with the people who are bullying him he will turn it against himself or someone else.

Helping your child cope with depression requires the same kind of approach as helping him deal with aggression.

First, don't get swept up in his feelings, but stay centred in your own. Second, don't allow him to treat you disrespectfully or thoughtlessly, even though he is obviously struggling. Anything that diminishes you makes you less able to help him, so you need to stick up for your own rights. Third, reflect back what he says to you, by answering with a question or agreeing, because that will give him an opportunity to clarify his feelings and express them more fully.

For example, if your child says, 'I hate my life', you might say, 'Are you really struggling at the moment?' or 'Yes, it is pretty tough for you just now'. The more he can explore his negative feelings the closer he will come to uncovering the underlying anger, so don't be tempted to deny his feelings by saying everything's fine, or it's not as bad as all that.

Don't try to make it all better by offering distractions or giving special privileges, which will be sending the message that not coping means you will cope for him. Avoid trying to bully him out of his feelings by saying he should pull himself together, he doesn't know how lucky he is, and so on.

However hard it is to live with a despairing child, there's no short cut back to happiness. He's in a process, and it has to run its course. Don't worry if it seems to be taking a long time – try to be patient.

People think of depression in wholly negative terms, which is a pity. You could just as well view it as a refuge in times of conflict or confusion, a safe space where people can go when the stresses of life are threatening to overwhelm them. A friend of mine used to call it Nature's way of making you stop and give your soul time to catch up. Maybe this is another reason why we've got an 'epidemic of depression' nowadays, because our pace of life has gone mad. Maybe it gives our bodies time to catch up and unwind too.

> Your depressed child needs to get in touch with his difficult feelings gradually, in his own time. This is inner work, and he may seem terribly remote. But you can help and support him enormously by just being there for him. Sitting and watching television together sometimes is companionable and very undemanding. Playing cards and board games or even doing jigsaws can be calming and constructive.

Drawing and painting and any sort of craft work are also good ways of occupying time, and if your child likes reading, make sure he's got a plentiful supply of library books. Try not to feel afraid of your child's unhappiness or you will make him frightened too. Accept it as a fact of life, and help him to live with it until it passes.

Depressed people can often gain strength from the natural environment. Simply feeling the earth beneath your feet, even in your own back garden, can be wonderfully grounding. If your child likes the countryside or parks, take him as often as you can, but don't expect him to be particularly sociable. Let him simply be with his own thoughts in Nature.

I know a child who suffered a number of terrible setbacks and became deeply depressed. All she wanted to do was to go up on the moors and walk. Her mother went walking with her as often as she could, and she gradually came through.

It goes against a parent's instincts to let a child suffer, but when your child is depressed that can be the best thing to do. Your depressed child needs lots of love and support, but he also needs space to experience his own feelings and learn how to cope with them himself. He doesn't need you to fight his battles, and that includes the inner battle against his own anger. His pain is showing that the anger is still alive, a glow among the embers,

Don't be panicked by your child's depression. Look upon it as his way of coming to terms with difficult feelings at a manageable pace. Don't try to rush him, but let him know that you are there for him if he wants to talk about anything.

Bouts of depression can often lift on their own, especially if you don't panic, but if you feel your child is sinking too deep or if he displays self-destructive tendencies, you might consider suggesting that he get some help from the doctor. There's a range of antidepressant drugs available now, designed to offer short-term relief from symptoms so that patients can feel more capable of getting on top of their problems. Your doctor may also want to arrange some kind of cognitive therapy alongside the drug treatment.

The important thing to bear in mind is this isn't a one-size-fits-all situation. People respond differently to different drugs, and some antidepressants have even been linked to an increase in negative symptoms in some patients. You need to give the drugs a few weeks to start to work, but after that, if your child isn't showing any improvement in his mood, you should talk to the doctor about changing his prescription. Good communication is the key.

The same thing goes for talking therapies. Your child will probably be offered a course of six sessions in the first instance, so the therapy will be very goal-focused and your child could make rapid progress, but if after a few weeks he doesn't seem to be getting much out of it, don't assume that this way of working just isn't for him – try a different therapist.

But what if your child becomes suicidal? Climbing out of upstairs windows, walking in front of cars, taking handfuls of painkillers – these are not unusual cries for help. It may comfort you to bear in mind that they very rarely result in suicide. But, of course, they must still be taken very seriously. Your child must be in desperate need to make such desperate cries for help.

I think it's more important than ever with a suicidal child to talk openly about what is going on. Explain to him the possible consequences of his behaviour – that suicide attempts can often result not in death but in drastic and crippling injuries, that most attempted suicides are profoundly grateful that they didn't die, that the dreadful moment passes and that thoughts of suicide can become a lifelong habit, so what starts as a refuge from problems can turn into a trap.

> Let him know you are always there for him if he ever wants to talk about anything that's troubling him. Tell him that if he would prefer to talk to a counsellor, you will arrange it for him. Discuss ways of coping with desperate feelings by letting them run their course, instead of panicking or trying to fight them. Help him to understand that time is the great healer, and that simply finding ways of passing time is one way of letting it do its work.

Last, but not least, be sure to tell him how absolutely terrible it would be for you to lose him. Say you don't want him to kill himself, but you realize there's nothing you can actually do to stop him. In this way, you are allowing your child to be responsible for himself. You are also being pragmatic, for there really isn't anything anyone can do to stop a person from committing suicide once they've made up their mind to it.

This is a frightening realization, but a vital one. A parent's first instinct when threatened with the loss of a child is to act – to take any measures, however desperate – to protect and save the child. When the threat comes from the child himself the parent's actions can be very counterproductive. You may find that you feel bewilderingly antagonistic towards your suicidal child, and more inclined to try to force him out of his depression than to give him the support he needs.

Be kind to yourself. Spread the burden of responsibility by talking to your doctor, even if your child absolutely refuses to accept treatment himself – you need someone to talk to as well. It's a volatile and alarming situation, but if your child feels suicidal he is getting very close to a breakthrough. The anger and hatred turned in upon the self has become so intense as to be murderous. The glow in the embers is about to burst into flame.

When your depressed child does manage to express anger, react positively so that he feels it's OK to be angry. Show him that you are not afraid of his anger, and he won't need to be afraid of it either.

Giving your child permission to be angry, whether he tends to turn it out against other people or in upon himself, depends upon your ability to protect your own boundaries. Helping your child to use his anger effectively will depend upon your ability to use your own.

There's a test you can do right now to see what your normal anger pattern is. Write this sentence five times, filling in the gaps: 'I get angry when . . . and then I . . .' For example, 'I get angry when they play loud music next door and then I thump on the wall / phone the police / want to cry.' Don't think about it at all; just put the first things that come into your head.

If you normally tend to react to angry feelings by getting aggressive or upset, you might well see the same pattern in your child. You could try the test on him and see if there's a similarity:

'My child gets angry when I ask him to do the dishes and then he sulks in his room for the rest of the evening.'

HOW TO USE ANGER EFFECTIVELY

You will probably have many opportunities to practise using anger effectively if your child is being bullied because however hard you try not to be swept along on his tidal wave of rage or despair you will certainly not succeed all the time. You will also have plenty of anger of your own – towards the people who are bullying him, the teachers who aren't protecting him and so on.

It's obvious that ranting and raving or wringing your hands is not going to help, but don't worry if you find yourself doing quite a bit of both. There isn't an easy, painless way of dealing with anger. It takes patience, courage, clarity and great effort to get it right, and most of the time we all veer slightly off-centre towards passive or aggressive patterns of avoidance.

Getting it right is much easier if you can adopt a positive attitude towards anger, and develop a clear strategy for dealing with it.

Adopting a Positive Attitude

It's easy to feel negative about anger because the negative effects of anger are generally more obvious than the good effects. One reason for this is that the good effects of anger are within the individual and the bad effects spill over on to other people.

When I was at school, for example, I did so badly in the

practice paper for my chemistry exam that my teacher told me I had no potential in the subject and should give it up straight away. I was angry because I had worked hard and done well in class up until then and I regarded my 12 per cent total in the practice paper as no more than a temporary hiccup. If I had kicked a few doors in and picked a fight with someone, or become depressed and withdrawn, these would have been very noticeable ill effects of anger. But, in the event, I simply refused to drop chemistry, revised well and got an A grade. Nobody else would have realized that this unexpected turnaround was purely because I was so outraged at being told I had no potential.

You can see anger at work all the time in sporting activities. If a football player feels he's the victim of a bad refereeing decision, for example, things could go in any of three ways: he might become aggressive and abusive, disrupting the game and risking being sent off; he might throw up his hands in disgust and stop trying, or he might use the extra adrenaline rush of anger to sharpen his concentration and make him more determined than ever to score a goal.

No footballer wants to fall victim to a bad decision, just as outside sport nobody wants to be unfairly treated, provoked or thwarted, but these things happen. Anger is an inevitable fact of life, and the difference between someone who is continually stressed and frustrated and someone who achieves his goals will often be no more than a clear strategy for dealing with it.

Developing a Clear Strategy

Here is a three-point plan for dealing with anger:

1. Feel it
2. Express it
3. Convert the energy into action

When it goes right, it's brilliant. For example, with my chemistry exam, I knew I felt angry, I told my teacher I was angry and I converted the energy into action by refusing to give up and going for an A.

Most of the time, of course, things are not so straightforward, and there can be problems and resistance at any stage. Sometimes we'll know we're angry, but express it negatively. Sometimes we'll be comfortable about expressing anger but then find it hard to do something positive about it. Quite often, we don't even get past the first post of recognizing that we feel angry.

1. Feeling angry

There are many reasons why we might not give ourselves permission to feel angry. This resistance can be internal, from guilt if our anger seems unreasonable, for example, or fear of being swept along by the sheer power of angry feelings. Or it can be more to do with how the person we are angry with might react. You won't want to upset a fragile child, for instance, and you won't want to enrage an aggressive one.

But that doesn't mean the anger just goes away. Energy is indestructible, and the energy of anger, if it isn't recognized and channelled into useful activities, can produce destructive physical, social and psychological effects.

The physical effects of anger, such as heightened blood pressure, which prepare the body for action, will cause physical problems if the anger is unresolved. In the long term, these might include heart disease, which is associated with an irascible temperament, and cancer, often linked to a passive one. In the short term, physical effects can include tension headaches, palpitations, breathlessness, skin disorders, aches and pains, and a whole range of other minor problems. Even being accident-prone can be a side effect of unresolved anger.

In a social context, anger is a way of asserting the self in relation to other people. In the long term, unresolved anger can disrupt relationships by making a person argumentative or withdrawn, unpredictable, unreliable, evasive or manipulative. Isolated incidents can cause rows over nothing and breakdowns in communication.

The psychological value of anger as a means of self-expression and self-preservation can also be lost when anger is unrecognized, and problems like depression, anxiety and low self-esteem can result.

Whenever you have a problem it's worth checking whether the hidden cause could be anger. If you have a headache or an accident or a nasty rash, try asking yourself, 'Why am I angry?' If you feel unhappy in a relationship, or if you feel sad for no obvious reason, ask yourself the same question. Really try to be open to all the possibilities, and you may be surprised at what comes up.

Another way to recognize anger, besides by its effects, is by learning its disguises. Words like 'disappointed', 'frustrated' and 'bored' can all be used to describe anger without naming it. Hurt, exasperated, concerned, amazed, bewildered . . . the list is endless.

Working in this way might help you to know, rationally, that you are angry. The next thing is to know it by feeling it. Angry feelings are very uncomfortable. They arise when there is conflict within the individual between what he's got and what he wants. As long as this conflict is unresolved, there will be some anxiety and frustration. People on both sides of the bullying situation have a low tolerance of frustration, and one of their problems is that they have to act or react instantly in order to avoid it. This means that as soon as they start to feel angry they must either get what they want immediately, or else immediately give up.

You can experience the energy of anger by making an anger line. Get ten pieces of paper and write one word on each that describes an angry feeling, for example, 'furious' and 'annoyed'. Lay them out on the floor in a line, starting with the mildest and finishing with the strongest expression of anger. Now stand beside one piece of paper, close your eyes and imagine that you are feeling 'furious' or 'annoyed' or whatever it says. Stand beside different parts of the anger line, noticing how different levels of anger energy feel. Be aware of your heart rate and breathing, and whether you are holding tension anywhere in your body. Feel the adrenaline rush and the power.

The trick, when it comes to handling anger, is not to react immediately by becoming instantly aggressive or depressed, but to hold back just long enough to give yourself time to choose how you want to react, and express your anger in more constructive ways.

So when you feel yourself getting a surge of anger, don't just lash out or crumble – hold on. Allow yourself to feel the energy. Buy time by:

- Taking a single slow breath – you can count to five as you breathe in and again as you breathe out if you find that helps
- Counting to ten under your breath
- Counting and naming five objects you can see: 'one, coffee mug; two, gel pen; three, budgie . . .'
- Describing five objects you can see: 'Broken kerb stone, green door, scrawny cat . . .'

Stopping, breathing, counting – this gives you time to register that you feel angry, to control the fight-or-flight impulse and to formulate how you want to express it.

2. Expressing anger

The most positive way of expressing anger is simply to say you feel angry. There's no need to worry about whether it's reasonable or not – you're describing a feeling, and feelings are not meant to be rational. When you can't tell the person you're angry with directly, acknowledging your anger to yourself will be enough to stop you having to deflect it on to yourself or someone else.

That's really all there is to it. As soon as you start using anger to force other people to change their behaviour or their opinions you turn a healthy form of self-expression into an act of aggression. Swearing, losing your temper, threatening and shouting are all aggressive ways of expressing anger, as, of course, is physical violence.

Other negative ways of expressing anger can be more oblique. Teasing is often a veiled form of aggression, even in the context of a loving family. When you tease someone, or are teased, listen to the actual words and not to the laughter. What's the literal meaning of what is being said? Would you say it in a serious voice?

Excessive criticism and shaming are also negative ways of expressing anger, as are coldness and rejection. So just say, 'I feel angry' and explain why. You don't have to justify feeling angry. You have a perfect right to your own feelings. What you don't have is the right to be right, or the right to get your own way.

If you feel you have to be right, that means you need someone to blame. In order for you to be right, the person you're angry with has to be wrong. Needing someone to blame puts you in a dependent position, and is a way of giving away your power.

In the same way, if anger is linked with getting your own way you become dependent on the person you are angry with to satisfy this need. Letting go of the right to be right also means letting go of the obligation to be right, and letting go of the right to have your own way also means letting go of the need.

It's in your own selfish interest to let go of blame and the desire to control because otherwise you can't release the energy that your anger generates and convert it into action.

3. Converting the energy into action

If you feel really, really angry you might have to start by taking the edge off it with some vigorous physical activity. Pillow-thumping is often recommended, or a brisk walk or run. Some people like to sing or dance to powerful music, like heavy rock or opera. Writing angry letters and painting angry pictures are also ways of riding the first wave of angry feelings. All these things will give you time to process your anger, to experience its power and to understand what it is that you need.

Why should you need time to understand your anger? Because, when it comes to angry feelings, things are rarely the way they seem. You may not be angry for the reason you think, or with the person you think, because when the anger you feel is too hot to handle it often gets deflected on to something or someone less threatening. You may not dare to be angry with your boss, for example, so you'll get really heated up about the political situation instead, or pick an argument with your partner.

Whenever you feel angry, particularly if the anger seems out of proportion, try asking yourself, 'What am I really angry about?' and 'Who am I really angry with?'

As well as being deflected from its true object in this way, anger can sometimes be used to disguise other uncomfortable feelings. You may not want to feel humiliated at getting lost, for example, so you'll become furious that the map isn't clear enough. Quite often, people get angry as a way of avoiding fear. So ask yourself, 'What am I afraid of?'

Say a man is angry with his wife for getting home late from a night out with her friends. What fears might his anger conceal? There's quite an array of answers.

If you ask yourself these questions whenever you feel angry, you will get some useful information about the situation you are in. If you notice a pattern – things that always make you angry – you will get some useful information about yourself. Do you get angry if you feel criticized? Are you afraid of being criticized? Why? Do you get angry if people ignore you? What would make you feel better?

Giving yourself time to understand your anger means you will be able to see what you need. Then you can use the energy of anger to start looking for ways of getting your real needs met.

WHEN ANGER GETS STUCK

Holding on to old anger keeps you locked in the past and wears you out. We say 'bearing a grudge' because a grudge is a burden. If you bear a grudge against someone it doesn't affect them in the least but it weighs you down and saps your energy. One way of getting rid of it is by forgiving.

Forgive . . . but Don't Forget

A lot of people don't want to forgive because they don't see why they should. The point about forgiveness is that you don't do it for your enemy's sake – you do it for yourself. It's not helpful to think 'Why should I forgive?' when you could change it to 'I can forgive; I have that power'. But don't forget. Hold on to the information your bad experience has given you (for example, how far you can trust someone) because that will keep you safe. Then you won't have to hold on to the pain and resentment, which may protect you from being hurt again but will also let the past poison the present and the future.

Forgiveness means breaking free of the past, including all the pain and fear, and living in the present moment. The ability to forgive can make a huge difference – the difference, in fact, between happiness and unhappiness – and yet it's a very quick and simple thing to do.

Furthermore, you only have to do it once. It's an act rather than a process. If old anger comes up again after it's done you just say to yourself, 'I've dealt with that, and it's in the past'.

There are different ways of making an act of forgiveness, but my favourite is this:

1. Remind yourself why you are doing it – that is, to free yourself from old angry feelings.
2. Write down all the things you need to forgive – 'You hit my child outside the school gate. You stole his mobile. You lied to the teacher and got him into trouble.'
3. Read through the list slowly and really let yourself experience the full force of your anger.
4. Let it go. It's in the past, and it's keeping you there.
5. Screw up the paper, or tear it up, and throw it in the bin. If you prefer, you could burn it or bury it. However you decide

to dispose of it, it's a good idea to express what this symbolic action means in words. You can make up your own formula. This is mine:

> I have decided to forgive you and put what happened in the past, where it belongs.
> I don't expect anything from you, or wish you any harm.
> In setting you free to get on with your life, I am freeing myself to get on with mine.
> So be it.

It may be a tall order to forgive the children who are bullying your child and you might like to practise on your family and friends first. Start with small things, like your partner forgetting to pick up the shopping on his way home, or your boss accusing you of something you didn't do. See how it feels to deliberately let go and forgive.

Don't forget that you can also forgive yourself for your own failings. Forgiving yourself is a way of boosting self-esteem because it helps you to accept your own weaknesses as well as strengths, and it will mean you feel less fearful of making mistakes in the future.

Forgiveness is a way of breaking your bonds and taking control of the situation. The first time your child is able to forgive his tormentors, even if it's just for one tiny insult or incident, he will understand that forgiveness is a way to power.

*

If your child is being bullied he is bound to feel angry. How he deals with his anger will depend partly on his temperament and partly on his past experience, but most of all it will depend upon how he sees you dealing with yours. If you tend to shout a lot he will tend to shout a lot; if you slam doors, he will slam doors; if you get physical, he will get physical.

Nobody can feel, express and use anger in positive ways all the time, but if you are always aware of the positive potential in anger you will be able to adopt a positive attitude towards it.

Anger is the root of power – the power to achieve, to succeed, to face healthy competition, the power to know and express the self. For a bullied child, it can be the power for overcoming fear.

RECAP POINTS

- If your child is being bullied he is bound to feel angry but he may not be able to express his anger in the bullying situation
- He may behave aggressively at home or turn his anger inwards and become depressed
- You can help your child by modelling safe ways of expressing anger and adopting a positive attitude towards it
- The ability to feel and express anger is an essential part of psychological self-defence

---

CHAPTER TEN

Dealing with Fear

Fear is a problem for every child who is being bullied.

By helping your child have enough confidence in you to tell you what's happening, you will have enabled her to overcome her fear of being exposed and shamed as a victim and her fear of having to cope on her own.

By helping her develop a more positive mental attitude you will have enabled her to overcome her fear that the bullying situation might take over her whole life.

By helping her recover her self-esteem you will have enabled her to overcome her fear that there might be something wrong with her.

By helping her experience and express her anger in constructive ways you will have enabled her to overcome her fear of standing up for herself.

Reducing the general level of fear in your child's life helps in two ways. First, it makes her less of a target for bullying as aggressive people are particularly drawn to fearful people, and second, it means she will be better able to focus on the particular fear of being bullied and deal with it effectively.

The first step in dealing with fear is simply to accept it. If your child is being bullied she's in a frightening situation and she's bound to feel afraid; don't try to protect her from that feeling. As fear is so infectious, you're bound to feel afraid too. Don't try to protect yourself.

This may seem blindingly obvious, but it isn't. Fear is such an uncomfortable feeling that most of us will go to great lengths not to feel it. Whenever we can, we disguise it, deny it and avoid it.

DISGUISING, DENYING AND AVOIDING FEAR

Disguising fear is about calling it something else. For example, say someone offers you free air tickets for a trip abroad and you're afraid of flying. You might tell yourself you're too busy, you haven't got anyone to go with or you don't want to feel beholden. In the bullying situation your child might disguise her fear of going to school by telling herself she feels ill or she's behind with her work. She might even be able to persuade herself that she's being clever by getting out of going to school because it isn't something you would normally allow her to do.

If she's willing to go to school but you're afraid of letting her go, you might disguise your fear by telling yourself she doesn't look well and she ought to stay at home. Or you might let her go, but find yourself walking down the road with her, as you just happen to have thought of something that means you are going the same way. You are acting out your fear, but not recognizing it as such.

Denying fear does not involve acting it out – it involves ignoring it altogether. When people deny their fear they become reckless and impulsive. They will accept the free air tickets even though they're terrified of flying, and then have a heart attack on the plane.

In the bullying situation, if your child denies her fear she might not bother to avoid risky places and situations; she might actually provoke the people who are bullying her. If you deny your fear, you might force her to go to school even though she's feeling ill or fragile. You might tell her to hit back, even though it's half the class that's picking on her.

Avoiding fear is about trying to create situations where you are protected from feeling afraid. Avoiders have a great need to be in control. They 'know their limitations'. They're 'realistic'. They wouldn't accept the free air tickets because flying really isn't their thing.

In the bullying situation, your child might try to avoid feeling fearful simply by staying at home. She might give up her outside interests and watch television instead. She might withdraw from her friendship group altogether in case they turn against her too. If you're avoiding your fear, you might encourage her to restrict herself like this so that you don't have to worry about her so much.

The problem with disguising, denying and avoiding fear is that it doesn't work. Most of us suffer levels of anxiety completely out of proportion to the actual dangers in our environment. Fear of illness, for example, is what drives people to see the doctor far more often than illness itself. It also causes them to make changes to their lifestyles that help to reinforce the anxiety by giving constant small reminders of it. Worrying about crime makes people prisoners in their own homes, even if no crime has ever actually been committed against them.

For your child, trying not to feel afraid is one of the things that will keep her locked into the bullying relationship. She will have to learn to face up to fear, to tolerate it and understand it, if she wants to be free.

FACING UP TO FEAR

What becomes clear when we stop running away from fear is that it's actually a very useful resource.

When we stop disguising it, it can give us information about ourselves. It shows us our limitations and therefore our opportunities for growth. Until someone can acknowledge it, she's like an alcoholic hiding her bottles – she has no chance at all of getting help and she can't move on.

When we stop denying fear, it can keep us safe. It can help us work within our boundaries, even while we are striving to push them back.

When we stop avoiding fear, we can let go of the need to control our environment with routines and rigidity. Decision-making is no longer a problem. We can embrace the future in a spirit of adventure, and savour the unexpected.

Without fear, we have no opportunity to experience ourselves as courageous and powerful. Facing up to fear and coming through it brings a feeling of elation. It's the perfect antidote for boredom and inertia, and it's also the root of success, dynamism and personal growth.

So don't be afraid of fear. Show your child how to face up to fear in a positive way. Don't doubt your own ability to cope, or hers. If you find yourself thinking you can't cope, just tell yourself firmly that you can. If you find yourself thinking your child can't cope, just tell yourself straight away that she can too.

Having a child who is being bullied is a frightening situation for parents and how you handle your anxiety will make a big difference. If you can't deal with your own fears they will add to the general level of fear surrounding the situation and make your child feel even more vulnerable and less supported. That's why it's important to look at your own attitudes towards fear and ensure you are handling it effectively yourself.

Start engaging with fear right now by:

- Thinking about the things you're afraid of
- Uncovering your secret fears
- Setting realistic challenges

Thinking About the Things You're Afraid of

The best way to do this is by writing a list. Try to get at least twenty things you're afraid of, just writing down whatever comes into your head, without censoring anything. It will probably be a mixed bag – for example, having a heart attack, walking into a room full of strangers, being alone at night, spiders, getting a big car bill . . .

Now consider each one in turn, putting a tick beside any that could represent a serious threat to life and limb.

Finally, check the ones you've ticked, asking yourself how likely they are to happen. What is the statistical chance of you being attacked at night or having a heart attack at your current age, for example? Are your biggest fears more likely to happen or more likely not to happen?

The function of fear is to keep you safe, and so if any of your fears aren't necessary for that – for example, there's no real risk to you in walking into a room full of strangers and the actual risk of you having a heart attack at forty-one is very low – then they are irrational fears. Irrational fears don't so much keep you safe as keep you small.

Most people have lots of irrational fears, including many they may not even be aware of.

Uncovering Your Secret Fears

Is there anything you'd like to do but somehow never seem to get around to? It could be something like trying yoga, for example, or eating at the new restaurant on the High Street or going to Japan or inviting your neighbour round for coffee. Write down five things you haven't got around to and add the reason why – 'I haven't done yoga classes because they never seem to be on at a convenient time'.

Examine each one carefully, asking yourself if there's any way you could actually be avoiding them out of fear. 'Well, I suppose I don't know what to wear to yoga classes and everyone might look down their noses at me because I'd probably be rubbish at it and I might not be able to find a parking space outside the hall . . .' You might find that your reasons are really excuses.

Now think about all the things you avoid doing because you just don't want to, such as driving into the town centre or using the internet. Write down a few and add the reasons you don't like doing them – 'I don't drive into town because it's easier to take the bus', 'I don't use the internet because I manage fine without it'. Examine your reasons and see if they could be masking unacknowledged fears. Are you nervous about driving in traffic, perhaps? Are you afraid you won't be able to find your way around the World Wide Web?

Think about the things your child has expressed an interest in doing but somehow never got around to. What were her reasons? What were yours? Could her fear have held her back, or could yours have made you overprotective?

Fear creates an invisible boundary around your life and one way of noticing it in all its disguises is by simply looking at the things you don't do, things that are outside your comfort zone.

Once you have identified your fears, you can start to tackle them by setting yourself some realistic challenges.

Setting Realistic Challenges

You can learn to handle big fears better by practising on smaller ones, building up your courage bit by bit the way you might build muscle in the gym. The trick is to start at the right level for your current capability. If you start with something too hard you'll end up feeling demoralized, but starting with something too easy will mean you aren't building up your courage at all.

Set yourself a task you're slightly afraid of doing. It has to be within your capability but outside your comfort zone, so you would normally prefer to avoid it. This might be something like calling someone who intimidates you, or eating alone in a restaurant, or wearing those green pointed shoes you bought and never had the courage to go out in. Choose a timescale, do it, and when you've done it, give yourself a reward.

Don't dismiss these small triumphs as meaningless on the grounds that most other people wouldn't find them scary. Fear is a personal thing, and therefore so is courage. Lots of things you take in your stride might be challenging to someone else. The point isn't what you do but the fact that it makes you feel scared and that you are willing to push through your fear.

As you gain confidence in the easiest things, try something slightly harder. Don't be overambitious – the important thing is that you feel the exhilaration of facing up to fear and overcoming it, a process perfectly described in Susan Jeffers's wonderful book, *Feel the Fear and Do It Anyway*.

Encourage your child to face her small fears in the same way so that she can have the experience of courage too. Supposing she's nervous around dogs, get your friend to bring his calm, completely un-alarming retriever round with him when he visits. Maybe the first time, your child will only manage to stay in the same room – don't push her. Respect her fear but give her opportunities to learn to handle it.

If your child is doubtful about whether to do something she finds scary, assess the situation and, so long as going for it will not put her in danger, don't discourage her.

People who see fear as a barrier limit their lives – seeing it as a challenge means you will be continuously pushing back your boundaries and your potential will be limitless.

Set yourself a small challenge every week and it will become your normal response to fear, so instead of automatically thinking, 'Help – I want to get out of here!' you'll be saying to life, 'Bring it on!' See if your child would like to do the same.

Doing lots of small challenges makes it feel more possible to tackle big scary ones. It can be helpful to share these with friends because you can keep each other on track, offer encouragement and join in the celebrations when you have reached 'mission accomplished'. You could have a challenges evening to set and discuss one big fear each one of you wants to confront within the next six months or year, and then meet again when the time's up to see how you've all got on.

Talking about challenges with your child will give you insights into what she really wants to achieve. This is the area where your support could be invaluable, because wanting something can be the best incentive for overcoming fear.

Facing up to fear is bound to be uncomfortable. Here are five simple techniques that could help you and your child to cope outside your comfort zone.

FIVE SIMPLE TECHNIQUES FOR MANAGING FEAR

Breathing

Fear can trigger the fight-or-flight response like anger, making you either lash out or cave in. Simply noticing your breathing is a good way of shifting your focus away from what's frightening you and back to yourself. It gives you time to feel the fear and make a decision about the best way of handling it. It helps you to achieve a degree of control.

As an added bonus, as soon as you notice your breathing you will automatically begin to regulate it, and calming your body will help to calm your fear.

You can count your breaths in and out, or try the other counting techniques I've suggested for tackling anger.

When the moment has passed, or if you suffer from general feelings of anxiety that strike quite randomly throughout the day, you can use focused, deep breaths to calm yourself.

Do this sitting or standing up straight. Start with a few slightly longer than normal breaths, breathing in slowly through your nose and sighing the breath out through your mouth. Then breathe in slowly and deeply, filling your lungs from the bottom up. Push your belly out first and then feel your whole chest expand right up to the top as you draw the air in.

Hold the breath for a count of three, and then slowly let the air out, starting from the top of your chest and finishing by pulling your stomach in. Take a few normal breaths and then repeat it, noticing how your body is feeling.

Focused breathing combines taking a deep breath with counting and you can use it any time you feel upset or agitated.

Finding Keepers

As well as focusing on breathing you can use a symbolic object, or 'keeper', to detach yourself from your fear. Some adults find this hard, but most children are very comfortable with it.

One of my children had a set of worry dolls, for example – she would confide one of her worries to each of them at night, and put them under her pillow. Then she could go off to sleep knowing that her worries were safe until she was ready to take them back in the morning.

My youngest daughter used a doll's teapot in the same sort of way. Every Friday she had a tables test at school, and every Thursday she couldn't sleep for worrying about it. Eventually, she had the idea of putting her anxiety in the teapot and closing the lid the night before tables tests. After that she was able to sleep well, she didn't wake up tired and she started to do much better. In a wonderful way, as she learned to worry less she actually had less to worry about.

Focusing on the Moment

Using keepers is an imaginative way of detaching from fear. A more rational way is focusing on the moment. Most fears are not about what is happening right now, but what might happen in the future.

If you're lying awake, worrying, you can detach by saying, 'Right now, nothing bad can happen so I'll put my fear on hold until the morning'. You might like to write your fear down, and then make the symbolic gesture of setting it aside. If you're having trouble concentrating on your work because you're afraid your child might be having a hard time at school, you can say, 'Right now, there's nothing I can do about it so I'll put my fear on hold until I get home'. If she doesn't feel like having a Sunday picnic because she's too busy worrying about what might happen at school during the week, tell her, 'Right now, today, there's nothing you can do about it, so why not have some time off from worrying?'

Powerful Objects

Throughout history people have used symbolic objects to give them good luck, courage, protection, calmness and clarity.

Journalists and film-makers reporting from war zones will often use powerful objects to protect them. Actors, sportspeople, climbers – people who have to face up to fear in their everyday life – will also use such objects. They may not necessarily be concrete things, like items of clothing or jewellery: they can be ritual activities or magic words, like mantras and affirmations.

Some people feel they work because they help you to focus your own energy. A good-luck charm, for example, simply shows you your own potential for good luck, and so magnifies it.

Others believe that certain objects are actually invested with particular powers you can draw on. Crystals are a case in point. If you're a sceptic, why not try this experiment: go to a crystals shop and just look around. Pick up any crystals you are attracted to, and see how they feel in your hand. Don't ask or read about particular qualities the different types of crystal are supposed to possess – trust your intuition. After you've made your selection, find out what uses your choice of crystal is recommended for. You may be surprised how accurately your intuition leads you towards the very crystal the books say that you need.

There's a whole ritual side to using crystals that children particularly enjoy – if they feel they're getting extra help from magical sources, this can stimulate their imagination and encourage creative thinking to tackle their problems. When you buy a crystal you start by cleansing it of all negative vibrations. There are lots of different ways of doing this, but here's one you might suggest:

Sit quietly with your eyes closed and the crystal in your hand. Take a few deep breaths. Imagine a flame of white fire emerging from the top of your head. Now draw the flame down to your brow, and then to your mouth. Blow the flame gently over your crystal three times.

The crystal is ready to be programmed with the purpose you want it to fulfil. This is simply a matter of voicing your intention.

It could be as general as 'Give me courage', or as particular as 'Help me to understand this piece of work'.

Crystals are satisfying objects as well as powerful ones. They can be beautiful to look at and good to hold. They carry the magic and mystery of the earth. Boys can keep a piece of polished crystal in their pockets; girls might prefer to wear one set in a ring or pendant.

It doesn't matter what sort of object you or your child choose to give you courage and calmness, and it doesn't matter why such objects work. The fact is that they do. Using objects in this way comes naturally to everyone – we face our first terrifying challenge of separation from our mothers by using transitional objects like teddies and comfort blankets. It's only in the Western world that believing in the extraordinary symbolic power of objects is dismissed as childish and superstitious.

Creative Visualization

We use visualization all the time in an involuntary way to understand reality. For instance, if I told you I was writing this in a converted stable at the bottom of my garden with my dog by my side, you would automatically create a mental picture of me, my stable, my garden and my dog.

Creative visualization is only different because it isn't involuntary. It means making mental pictures deliberately to create the reality you want.

There's nothing difficult about creative visualization. It's easy and enjoyable. You simply sit quietly for a few moments with your eyes closed, and relax. Take three or four slow, deep breaths to ease yourself out of your objective situation and into your inner space.

Now choose an image that will trigger the sort of emotion you want to feel. For instance, if you're afraid, you might choose to imagine a lion, an animal so strong and fearless that he can lie down on his back in the open and sleep.

Set the scene, imagining it as fully as you can, using all your senses. Feel the hot African sun; smell the dry air; see the red earth, the orange sun, the yellow grass; hear the breeze rustling through it, and the birds flapping up.

Now look at the lion, massive and majestic, moving slowly. Be the lion. Feel his feelings. In this way you can experience fearlessness and power without even getting out of your chair, and if you practise the visualization often you will be able to conjure up those feelings instantly by just thinking of the lion, not having to build the whole picture every time.

Visualization is a personal thing, like fear itself, and you need to work with images that particularly appeal to you. I like lions, but some people might prefer to work with elephants or giraffes or some other large animal that is well able to protect itself and doesn't have to worry about being eaten. Other people might favour dinosaurs.

If animals don't do it for you, you might like to try visualizing yourself as a superhero, feeling what it's like to have super powers that make you invulnerable. Or you could choose a real person you admire, imagining how it feels to be as brave as them, or someone fictional like the wonderful unflappable Marge Simpson.

Imagining yourself being brave is like a rehearsal. It gives you the experience of courage, making it feel more real and possible. It opens up that area of yourself so that you can move more readily into it.

You can use visualization in the same way when you are thinking about your child. How you picture your child will make a great difference to how you feel about her and therefore how she feels about herself. If you picture her as a small, frightened, sensitive person in a hostile environment, you will be full of fear for her and your fear will undermine her confidence in herself. You can elect to change the mental image you have of your child, and see her as the powerful, unique person she is.

Just for interest, try this in more general ways. If you want your child to be more polite, for example, make a point of always visualizing her as the polite child she can be. You will feel differently about her, she will feel differently about herself and that will have an effect upon the way she behaves.

You might like to try creative visualization in other relationships as well. A friend of mine was bullied by her elderly mother. Whenever the old lady started on one of her tirades my friend would picture a pink bubble floating down from the sky, growing larger as it fell, and finally engulfing her mother and containing her. Because pink, for my friend, was symbolic of love, this made it possible for her to separate herself from her mother in a loving way.

When my friend could no longer be provoked, her mother gradually gave up trying to provoke her, and they were able to discuss their differences more calmly and reasonably.

Some people like to visualize a star or a point of light just above their heads, protecting them, bringing them good luck and showing the way. A guardian angel could produce the same feelings of safety and power.

Techniques like these can help you tolerate the discomfort of fearful feelings without being overwhelmed and therefore to gain some mastery over them. Another way of tackling fear is with its powerful antidote – love.

THE POWER OF LOVE

Because fear is such a dreadful feeling, we hate and resent people who make us feel afraid.

Hating people gives them power over us because hatred is corrosive – it eats into our lives. We are diminished by it, just as those we hate are made disproportionately important. Hatred is both a cause and consequence of fear.

But loving people is empowering because when you are the one doing the giving you are the one who is in control. Fear cannot coexist with love, and so loving your enemy is the perfect antidote to fear. The problem is how can this apparently impossible goal be attained?

Years ago, I read about a man who had been imprisoned by the military junta in Greece and beaten so severely that his whole body looked like raw liver. Not a square inch of skin remained its normal colour.

The man didn't make a full physical recovery, but when he was well enough to talk about his appalling ordeal he said he did not hate the people who had beaten him – he pitied them.

I remember finding this story very hard to believe. How could anybody who had suffered such pain and terror at the hands of others not feel full of hatred and hungry for revenge?

It seems to me now that the answer is this – his injuries were so dreadful that if he had allowed himself to feel the huge hatred they could have inspired he would have been utterly over-whelmed by it and the rest of his life effectively destroyed. Love could be seen, in such extreme circumstances, as a sort of instinct for survival. Through love, and his own inspiring strength of character, the man was able to break free from his tormentors and create a new life for himself.

Most people never have to experience such extremes of fear and helplessness, so they don't have to learn to protect their lives from being eroded by hatred through the transforming power of love. It seems too hard, and they prefer to accept a degree of fear and resentment as an inevitable part of life.

But if your child is being bullied you may have such shock-ingly murderous feelings towards the people who are hurting and threatening her that you are willing to try quite radical methods of defusing your rage.

If you have been following some of the ideas in this book you will already have made a start on the incredible work of loving your enemies. You will have stopped judging them, by letting go of blame and guilt; you will have accepted them as they are, by not expecting them to change, but rather being prepared to take responsibility for making changes in yourself; you will have practised loving for the simple joy of loving, without needing any return, and you will have experienced the release that comes from forgiving.

If really loving your enemies is a step too far for you and your child, try pretending. See what happens when you behave towards them in a consistently polite and positive way, as if you regard them as friends. Put the energy of your anger and fear into creating a fabulous pretence, because friendliness will be exactly what they don't want or expect from you. Making you fear and hate them is their power and by rising above hatred, you win.

Damian

Damian got off on the wrong foot with his new science teacher and he could do nothing right. His teacher picked on him all the time, forcing him to answer questions and then ridiculing everything he said, using sarcasm to humiliate him in front of his friends.

Damian talked to his head of year about it, but that made matters worse, and it felt as if there was nothing he could do but sit and take it. This made him hate his science teacher even more and he spent most of his science lessons scowling and muttering at the back – which gave his teacher even more to mock him for.

Then Damian hit on a new idea. He would pretend that he liked his science teacher. He went into science with his head up and shoulders back, and smiled at her warmly as he found a seat near the front. When his teacher put him on the spot, he said brightly that he didn't know the answer and when she ridiculed him for not knowing, he agreed affably that science probably wasn't his strongest suit.

Damian's teacher was perplexed. His reasonableness and

resolute niceness disarmed her. She knew she was being played, but now she was the one who could do nothing about it.

Pretending to love your enemies is an interesting starting point because it can be like pulling a single thread and watching the cloth unravel. Being nice to them takes away their power, and when they have less power they seem less frightening, and when you fear them less you hate them less . . . which means you're moving towards really loving your enemies.

If your child is being bullied, she is certainly going to experience fear, and you are probably going to feel afraid too, on her behalf. The only way you can avoid being overprotective, which could prevent her from dealing with her fear effectively, is by dealing effectively with your own.

Dealing effectively with your fear means first of all acknowledging that you feel afraid, and then using whatever methods you need to help you not let your fear stop you from getting on with your own life and letting your child get on with hers.

If you can try to live less fearfully in all areas of your life, you will be providing a good role model for your child. You will be helping her to see that even something as apparently negative as fear can carry valuable lessons about courage and love.

RECAP POINTS

- If your child is being bullied she is bound to feel afraid – and so are you
- Fear is uncomfortable so we often try to deny, disguise or avoid it
- Facing up to your fear means you won't be adding to the general level of anxiety and provides a strong model for your child
- You and your child can build up to handling big fears by practising on smaller ones first

CHAPTER ELEVEN

How Helping Your Child Can Bring Insights for You

Working through the ideas in this book with your child may lead you to share some surprising insights into your family life and attitudes. It may also bring insights that are particularly about you, about the amazing business of being a parent and about the broader social context of your life.

THE HIDDEN HERITAGE

When you discover how much you can help your child take control of his situation and rise above it simply by being a positive, confident and assertive role model, you are bound to ask yourself sooner or later, 'Could it have been victim feelings and attitudes in me that made him vulnerable in the first place?'

Having a child who is being bullied makes you a victim too. It can reawaken painful victim feelings in you that date back to your own childhood. Experiences of helplessness, rage and terror can be overwhelming in childhood, and children learn to develop coping mechanisms that sidestep or disguise their difficult feelings if they are not helped to resolve them. In this way, such feelings become invisible.

For example, childish insecurity can harden into inflexibility in adult life, helplessness can turn into a need for control and low self-esteem can lead to patterns of self-sabotage and under-achievement. Children who don't learn to handle their anger in positive ways can become depressed or antisocial adults, and those who have problems with fear can learn to feel safe by making their own lives small.

Besides such unconscious adaptations there are also unconscious attitudes that run through families like an underground stream, surfacing in automatic responses to life which can be positive or negative, optimistic or pessimistic, judgemental or accepting. These attitudes seem normal and therefore sensible, inevitable even, and many people go through life never noticing that there are other equally valid ways of seeing and understanding things, ways that could be more conducive to feelings of happiness and wellbeing.

Having a child who is bullied gives parents a second chance to recognize and resolve victim issues in themselves, this time with adult help – their own. It's a painful business, but the good news is that simply recognizing these unconscious issues is enough. As soon

> as they become conscious, they stop having a negative influence in your life and are no longer a hidden heritage for your children.

THE MAGIC MIRROR

When you see that your child's victim attitudes could have contributed to his situation, and that those attitudes could have filtered through to him from you, you may begin to wonder if there are other unconscious issues you are passing on to your children without even being aware of it.

The good news is you can see something of what these are simply by looking at your child. Children live out their parents' unlived lives, and so they are like magic mirrors, showing us the secret side of ourselves.

Suppose your child has a terrible problem with shyness. You may not be aware of any such problem in yourself because you have learned to adapt to it. You avoid challenging social situations, perhaps, or have found ways of disguising your discomfort. But the fact that your child has this problem could point to an unresolved issue in you. If you recognize it and address it in yourself, you will not only break free of the limiting adaptive behaviour you've developed over the years, you will also find that it stops being a problem for your child.

If you find the idea that children mirror what we can't see in ourselves quite hard to take, it might be easier to see it in other families first. Notice what your friends say about their children.

'Jamie's so stubborn!'

'Andrea's so wilful!'

'If only Simon weren't so shy!'

Jamie's mum might not think of herself as stubborn, or Andrea's as bossy, and Simon's dad might not see himself as shy, but these things could well be glaringly obvious to their friends.

You might say, 'I haven't got any problems!' But everybody has problems; everybody needs problems, or they wouldn't be able to grow. People who think they haven't got any problems are simply projecting them on to someone else.

Supposing, for example, you're afraid of the dark, but you can't face the fear and deal with it. If you project your fear on to your child, and he becomes afraid of the dark, two things happen. First, you feel confident in comparison with your child, and second, you can protect yourself from experiencing darkness by leaving the hall light on all night under the guise of helping your child.

In a family situation, one sensitive child can carry the whole family's unacknowledged problems. Having a child who is identified as the cause of all the family's anger, anxiety, shame or disappointment, means that the real causes don't have to be examined. Children like these are the black sheep in otherwise functional families. They are often called 'difficult', which is the word Alan Train uses in his excellent book, *The Bullying Problem – How to Deal with Difficult Children* (Souvenir Press, 1995), to describe both victims and bullies.

Parents of 'difficult' children may have a particular need to find ways of acknowledging their own difficulties and taking responsibility for them. They may need to find out as much as they possibly can about the dark side of themselves.

SEEING THE SHADOW

A child learns by what his parents are, rather than what they do. The problem is that no one knows exactly what they are, because beyond the known, conscious area of the self, there is a whole vast unconscious hinterland.

Imagine your life is a film. You're producing it, directing it, acting in it and trying to make it just the way you want it to be. All the bits you don't like finish up on the cutting-room floor, and you forget about them. You don't even remember exactly what they are.

But that's not the end of the story because when a child comes along he will inherit not only the conscious, accepted parts of his parents' personalities but all the unconscious parts as well. His life's film includes all the censored and rejected reels from yours. Sorting through your unwanted stuff uses up your child's energy and resources, and stops him getting on with the creative task of realizing his own potential.

> The most empowering thing you can do as a parent is to have another look through all the stuff on the cutting-room floor. By trying to rediscover the parts of yourself that you may have rejected, or uncover the parts of yourself you may never have realized, you will be creating more balance in your own life and leaving less unfinished business for your child to tidy up.

Everybody has the potential to be everything. As John Lennon put it, we're all Hitler and we're all Jesus. If you see yourself as entirely hard-working and conscientious, you may be overlooking your capacity for laziness and impulsiveness, and these will become an issue for your children. They may become driven, like you, or completely lacking in drive, but unless they manage to achieve the balance in their lives that you have not achieved in yours, they will pass the same either-or choices on to their own children.

You can gain access to the cutting-room floor of your own unconscious in lots of ways without having to go into therapy or dream interpretation. All the information is there in your day-to-day life. It's just a question of learning how to see it.

Carl Jung called the unconscious side of the self the 'shadow'. The fact that it is unconscious means that you can't see it in any direct way – you can only glimpse its reflection. As soon as you understand that what you are seeing is your own shadow, it stops being unconscious and falls under your conscious control. This process is sometimes called withdrawing projections.

Glimpsing your shadow is easy if you know where to find it, and have the courage to look.

First of all, of course, you can look at your child. What are his problems? They could be yours. What are his strengths? They could be your unrealized dreams and potential. It isn't only faults and flaws we consign to the unconscious. It can be good things that we perhaps didn't recognize as such, like creativity, for instance, if we grew up in a family system that valued conformity. It can be qualities that children are often told off for – like wilfulness and pride – which can actually underpin success in adult life.

Now look at the people you know. Think of the three people you dislike the most, and write down their names. Taking one at a time, list all the things you dislike about them. When you've done that, think of the three people you like the most, and list all the things you like about them. You have listed your own unacknowledged faults and strengths.

One of the things that I discovered when I did this was that I was unreliable. I couldn't believe I'd never realized it before. I was always promising to go places and do things, only to change my mind at the last minute. If I'd noticed it at all I'd put it down to natural exuberance – I just couldn't say no – or just plain busyness. Being aware of the problem means I don't make so many promises these days, and when I do promise to do something I make a conscious effort to stick to it.

Here are some other ways of getting a glimpse of your shadow:

Slips of the Tongue

When you say something you didn't mean . . . your shadow did. This is what's popularly known as a Freudian slip, though because the professor himself was so obsessed with sex most people only notice them when they're directly sexual.

When you have a slip of the tongue, consider what it might say about you, and why you don't want to recognize it.

Actions with Unwanted Consequences

If you do something that accidentally upsets someone, or disrupts something, ask yourself, 'What is it in me that wanted this outcome? Why am I reluctant to admit it?'

Supposing you arrive late for a dinner party, the hosts are stressed and the food's gently drying out in the oven. You probably feel genuinely sorry and have a really good excuse, but put those things aside and ask the above questions – especially if it's not the first time that has happened.

Ask the same questions also if you inadvertently do something that delights someone or makes something possible.

Things People Say About You

If someone criticizes you, resist the temptation to react defensively, and treat what they say as a possible piece of useful information. This is not to say they're right – just that there might be a grain of truth in what they say.

Similarly, if someone praises you, resist the temptation to dismiss it out of hand. They could be showing you something great about yourself that you find it hard to acknowledge.

Physical Ailments

The psychological aspect of physical symptoms is widely accepted these days. Most ailments have obvious verbal connections, which can be worth noticing. We use the word 'headache', for example, as a synonym for 'problem'. If you've got a pain in the neck, what or who is being a nuisance? If you suffer from stomach trouble, what is it that you can't stomach?

Look at the effects of your physical symptoms. Do you get a lot of colds and infections which keep you away from other people? Perhaps you have a strong unconscious need for more personal space and time to be on your own. If you make that conscious, and take the time you need, you may find that you stop getting all the bugs that are going round.

Consider the timing too. What was going on in your life when you developed a specific health problem? If it's something that recurs, what seems to trigger it? Sometimes your body speaks your secret mind.

Humour

When you joke about something, look at the actual words you use. What do they mean, joking aside? We know that teasing can be a way of masking aggression, but humour can also mask a whole range of other unacknowledged attitudes. Self-deprecating jokes, for example, may express a person's deepest fears and suspicions about himself.

Think about the things that make you laugh. Is your humour dark, cruel, racist, scatological, silly, homophobic? What information does that give you about yourself? Remember this isn't about judging yourself – it's simply about becoming more aware.

Opposites

Every emotion contains the potential for its opposite. Couples who have been passionate partners in marriage can become bitter enemies in divorce.

Think of all the people and things you feel strongly about, and imagine that you hold the opposite view. What would this tell you about yourself? Why is it something you don't want to know?

Seeing the shadow side of yourself is really just a question of being open to other possibilities besides the way things look. It's about seeing yourself the way you don't want to see yourself, as well as the way you do. It doesn't happen all at once because no one can ever uncover all there is to know about himself. It comes in moments of insight, which can be traumatic.

If you want to try opening up to all your possibilities, you will need to approach it in a non-judgemental way, and be ready to give yourself all the love and forgiveness you need.

Why would you put yourself through it? Because it can be wonderfully liberating. When you know the worst about yourself you aren't vulnerable to criticism from anyone – yourself or other people. You don't have to invest so much energy in defensive manoeuvres, and life feels nicer because you aren't projecting so much of your own dark side on to everything around you.

PARENTING THE INNER CHILD

Another way of uncovering your hidden agendas is called 'inner child' work. The idea here is that we all carry inside ourselves the child that we once were. Our unresolved childish feelings can be reactivated by events in later life, and this in turn sets up a sort of instant replay of all the things our parents said to us in similar circumstances when we were little.

According to this scheme of things, we each have three inner voices – the inner child, the inner parent and the mature adult.

The inner child will usually express himself in terms of feelings because children are emotional beings – they haven't learned to rationalize and detach themselves from their emotions. The parental voice is usually critical. The inner child might say things like, 'It's not fair', 'Why should I?' and 'You don't like me'. The inner parent will be more on the lines of 'Don't be silly', 'Act your age' and 'Stop whining'.

If your parents were particularly controlling, your inner dialogue might run something like this:

CHILD: I want to go out.
PARENT: No, you don't *or* Well, you can't.
CHILD: I don't want to go out.
PARENT: Yes, you do *or* Well, you've got to.

Your behaviour will be self-sabotaging because whenever you want something it triggers the parental veto, and the parent in you will not allow you to have it.

As long as this pattern is unconscious, you have to go on

acting it out, and something will always stop you getting what you want. Noticing the parent–child dialogue means you can intervene – in the mature adult voice.

Supposing you want a holiday. Your inner child says, 'I want a holiday!' Your inner parent says you can't. Now bring in your mature adult. Acknowledge the child's feelings, and take them seriously. Then, even if you decide you really can't go this time – because you're low on cash, for example – you are breaking the 'I want / You can't' connection by introducing a third point of view, 'Perhaps it will be possible'.

As your children grow, they will trigger feelings in you that you experienced at different stages of your own childhood, and your first reaction will be to go automatically into your parent voice. Noticing when you sound like your parents, and introducing your own mature adult point of view, will be helpful whenever your children challenge you.

This isn't to say that your parents were not good parents. Part of the role of parenting is to socialize children, to set limits and temper the child's natural egocentricity, and there's no perfect way of doing it. Your parents' messages were influenced by the social mores of the time, their own experience of growing up and the unique combination of your temperament with theirs. They will have done their best for you, using the knowledge they had, but you live in different times and you can add to that sum of knowledge, just as your children will add to yours. In this way, parents mature and grow through the experience of parenting. It's evolution.

There are lots of books about inner child work if you want to go into it in depth, but in the meantime here's a simple exercise.

Many counsellors use it with clients of every description, although it was originally devised by Penny Parks for victims of abuse in childhood. It comes from her book *Rescuing the Inner Child* (Souvenir Press, 1990).

1. List half a dozen childhood experiences that you remember as being upsetting or disturbing.
2. Choose one of them.
3. Write a letter from the adult you to your inner child, asking him/her to describe what happened.
4. Write a letter from your inner child, describing the event. Take enough time to really think yourself back into it. (Have a tissue handy!)
5. Write thanking your inner child for sharing that horrible experience. Sympathize. Give the mature adult point of view. Tell your inner child that you will always be there to offer love and support whenever he/she needs it.
6. Write a rescue scene. Go with your inner child into the experience and then do whatever you like to protect him and save him/her. You can be as violent as you like! You can have superhuman strength! You can fly! Make it as epic and dramatic as you want to, and enjoy it.

Looking for the shadow and getting to know your inner child are ways of finding out things you didn't know about yourself, or had forgotten. The better you know yourself the less of your unseen baggage your child will have to carry, and the more he will be able to be his own authentic self.

This work will not only bring you insights into yourself and your family. It will also uncover things you may not have noticed before about your whole social environment.

A BULLYING ENVIRONMENT

Asking yourself, when things go wrong, 'What does this tell me about myself?' and 'What changes can I make in myself to resolve it?' is the way to turn your problems into opportunities. It's how not to be a victim.

When you start working in this way you may be surprised to notice that taking personal responsibility goes very much against the social grain.

Whenever there's an accident, a disaster or even a simple mistake, everyone looks for someone to blame. Children who fail are taking their schools to court. Sick people are suing their doctors. The man in the street blames the politicians, and the politicians blame each other.

When we aren't blaming other people, we're blaming our situation. We're encouraged to believe that our wellbeing depends upon external criteria – we need to have the right car, job, house, in order to be happy. Instead of taking responsibility for our own happiness by learning to value what we've got, we blame what we haven't got and stay dissatisfied. As soon as we get one thing, we go on to want another. In this way we make ourselves the helpless victims of circumstance.

Besides always looking for something that will make us happy, we are encouraged to expect instant gratification for all our needs, and this attitude erodes our capacity for tolerating frustration, which is one of the problems bullies and victims share.

And we are so full of fear! We're afraid of illness, unemployment and crime, of commitment and divorce, of parenthood and childlessness, of death. The prevailing attitude is not to face up to fear with a muscular acceptance of the way things are, but to manipulate circumstances so that we can avoid it.

In these and many other ways, the world we live in can make victims of us all. But here's the good news. Social change starts from the individual. When you change your own attitudes you will see an instant knock-on effect in the attitudes of your family and friends. As they in turn change, the people around them will be affected too. The butterfly flapping its wings eventually has an effect, even on the far side of the globe.

RECAP POINTS

- Helping your child to handle victim feelings can give you insights into your own unconscious attitudes
- Seeing the dark side of yourself can be both challenging and liberating
- Becoming conscious of your hidden faults and fears means they stop being part of your child's hidden inheritance

CONCLUSION

Your Powerful Child

In the past few years, bullying has become a big concern for parents, children, schools and even the government. Frightening changes have been taking place, and it can feel as if we are struggling to keep up with them.

First, there's the sheer volume of the problem, with the vast majority of children in schools now saying they have been bullied; there's the disappearance of gender stereotypes, with girls doing as much physical bullying as boys; there's the increased brutality of reported cases, and the rising number of children who carry weapons.

Then there's the proliferation of new forms of bullying using modern technology, which can invade every area of a child's life and cause humiliation on a massive scale.

But the situation may not be as dark as it seems because at the same time, schools are developing ever more sophisticated methods of tackling bullying:

- Raising awareness with things like circle time, bullying theme days and drama workshops
- Initiatives such as peer support schemes, counselling and bully-boxes
- Security systems such as closed-circuit television
- Creative interventions like the no-blame approach

Furthermore, where strong sanctions are needed, the government is about to give teachers statutory powers to punish children who bully and take action against parents who refuse to support the school.

Physical bullying is usually dealt with effectively in school and cases that involve weapons or extreme violence are still so rare as to make the national news. Far and away the most common form of bullying is teasing and name-calling, which is much more difficult for schools to deal with.

As a parent, you might find that reassuring because you are probably most worried about your child being injured in a bullying incident, but children themselves say that being taunted or excluded can actually hurt more and be harder to cope with, and whatever form the bullying takes the only real damage is virtually always psychological.

Some people are naturally more resilient than others, but even the most confident can be crushed by persistent bullying, and the longer it goes on, the less capable they will be of brushing it off, and the more appealing they will become as victims.

The immediate psychological effects of bullying are loss of

self-esteem and self-confidence, unhappiness, anxiety, and anger or depression. There may be problems with concentration, reduced school performance, disrupted friendships, psychosomatic ailments and feelings of hopelessness and despair. In the worst cases, being bullied can drive a person to violent revenge or suicide.

In some people, the effects of childhood bullying can carry over into adult life leading to long-term patterns of self-doubt, self-dislike and self-sabotage. But in others, the experience can strengthen their determination to succeed and not be beaten down.

In the government report based on research carried out by ChildLine, 'Tackling bullying: listening to the views of children and young people', the only three things that children thought might be effective were avoiding the bullies, staying close to your friends and learning to stand up for yourself. The first two are obviously not always possible, so of those three, learning to stand up for yourself was the only one that children thought would 'always or nearly always work'.

By standing up for yourself children don't mean hitting back, since most bullying is non-physical – they mean refusing to get upset, letting other people's nastiness be like water off a duck's back, so that it's their problem, not yours.

Parents are in a unique position to help children develop good psychological self-defence. It isn't a quick-fix solution, but such a thing doesn't always exist when it comes to bullying situations. This approach requires effort and commitment, but it's also entirely risk-free – and it works. If the bullying is non-physical, it may be enough all on its own – if the bullying involves gangs or violence, good psychological self-defence may give you and your child the clarity and courage you need in order to get help.

When your child is bullied, she needs more than ever the powerful experience of being loved unconditionally. As long as you want her to change – to be less unhappy, less vulnerable, less fearful, more assertive, more outgoing, less angry – you are not accepting her just as she is.

But making changes in yourself – not letting her situation overwhelm you but making yourself happier, less fearful and so on – and mirroring them for your child is an act of unconditional love. It will bring the changes in your child that you are looking for, without carrying any element of rejection.

Love is one thing that gives a child power; the other is knowledge. Your child needs to know:

- That although she can't choose the way people behave towards her, she can choose how she responds
- That although she can't choose the events that happen in her life, being happy is a positive personal choice

- That she is a unique and wonderful person, with exactly the same rights as everybody else
- That she can use the power of her anger to protect herself, without having to attack anybody else
- That fear is the only way to experience courage, and facing up to fear is the only way to grow

If your child can learn these lessons, they will not only help her to be less vulnerable and afraid of bullying, which in turn will mean she's a less satisfying victim and the bullies will move on; they will also help her to be less vulnerable and afraid of everything, and this will enable her to reach her full potential in all the different areas of her life.

Further Reading

For children age nine-plus

Alexander, J., *Bullies, Bigmouths and So-called Friends*, Hodder, 2006

Alexander, J., *How 2 B Happy*, A and C Black, 2006

Alexander, J., *The Seven-day Bully-buster*, Hodder, 2007

Alexander, J., *The Seven-day Self-esteem Super-booster*, Hodder, 2007

Kaufman, Gershen et al. – *Stick Up for Yourself – Every kid's guide to personal power and positive self-esteem*, Free Spirit Publishing, 1999

For adults

Abrams, Jeremiah and Zweig, Connie (eds.), *Meeting the Shadow – The hidden power of the dark side of human nature*, Penguin Putnam Inc., 1991

Biddulph, Steve, *Raising Boys: Why boys are different – and how to help them become happy and well-balanced men*, HarperCollins, 2003

Biddulph, Steve and Sharon, *The Complete Secrets of Happy Children: A guide for parents*, HarperCollins, 2003

Bradshaw, John, *Creating Love*, Piatkus, 1992

Burns, Dr David, *Ten Days to Great Self-esteem*, Vermillion, 2000

Harris, Thomas, *Staying OK*, Arrow, 1995

Hastings, Julia, *You Can Have What You Want*, Touchstone, 1992

Hay, Louise, *You Can Heal Your Life*, Eden Grove Editions, 1988

Hay, Louise, *The Power is within You*, Eden Grove Editions, 1991

Holbeche, Soozi, *The Power of Gems and Crystals*, Piatkus, 1989

Jampolsky, Gerald, *Love is Letting Go of Fear*, Celestial Arts, 1979

Jeffers, Susan, *Feel the Fear and Do It Anyway*, Arrow, 1991

Katie, Byron, *Loving what is*, Rider, 2002

Further Reading

Lawrence, Anne and Denis, *Self-Esteem and Your Child – A guide to happy parenting*, Minerva Press, 1996

Lindenfield, Gael, *Confident Children – A parent's guide to helping children feel good about themselves*, Thorsons, 1994

Madow, Leo, *Anger – How to Recognise and Cope with it*, Allen & Unwin, 1972

Parks, Penny, *Rescuing the 'Inner Child'*, Souvenir Press, 1990

Peck, M. Scott, *The Road Less Travelled*, Arrow, 1990

Robinson, Bryan, *Heal Your Self-Esteem*, Health Communications Inc., 1991

Seligman, Martin, *Authentic Happiness – Using the new positive psychology to realise your potential for lasting fulfilment*, Nicholas Brealey Publishing Ltd, 2003

Sher, Barbara, *Self-esteem Games – 300 fun activities that make children feel good about themselves*, John Wiley and Sons, 1998

Skynner, Robin, *Family Matters*, Methuen, 1995

Tolle, Eckhart, *The Power of Now*, Hodder and Stoughton, 1999

On creative self-expression

Edwards, Betty, *Drawing on the Right Side of the Brain – How to unlock your hidden artistic talent*, HarperCollins, 1993

Gawain, Shakti, *Creative Visualization*, Bantam, 1982

Goldberg, Nathalie, *Writing down the Bones – Freeing the writer within*, Shambhala Publications Inc., US, 2006

McNiff, Shaun, *Art as Medicine – Creating a therapy of the imagination*, Piatkus, 1992

For children age nine plus:

Alexander, J., *How to be a Brilliant Writer*, A and C Black, 2005

Hughes, Ted, *Poetry in the making*, Faber and Faber, 1986

On bullying

Lawson, Sarah, *Helping Children Cope with Bullying*, Sheldon Press, 1994

Mains, Barbara and Robinson, George, *Stamp Out Bullying*, Lucky Duck Publishing, 1991

McLeod, Mary and Morris, Sally, *Why Me? Children Talking to ChildLine about Bullying*, ChildLine, 1996

Tattum, Delwyn and Herbert, Graham, *Bullying – A positive response. Advice to parents, governors and staff in schools*, CHIE, 1990

Train, Alan, *The Bullying Problem – How to Deal with difficult children*, Souvenir Press, 1995

USEFUL ADDRESSES

British Association for Counselling and Psychotherapy

BACP House
35–37 Albert Street
Rugby CV21 2SG
Send an A5 SAE for a list of counsellors and counselling organizations in your area or visit www.bacp.co.uk

Education Otherwise

36 Kinross Road
Leamington Spa
Warwickshire CV32 7EF
Tel: 01926 886828
Support for parents educating their children at home

HELPLINES

ChildLine

Tel: 0800 1111
Lines are open 24/7.
Calls are free and don't show up on itemized phone bills from land lines, 3, BT Mobile, Fresh, O2, Orange, TMobile, Virgin and Vodaphone.

Telephone counselling for children, or they can text 0800 400 222 between 9.30 a.m. and 9.30 p.m. on weekdays or 9.30 a.m. to 8 p.m. at weekends.

Samaritans
Tel: 08457 909090
Local telephone numbers in your local directory.
Calls are charged at local rates.
Counselling for older children and adults, mostly by phone, but sometimes face to face if preferred, or you can email jo@samaritans.org

WEBSITES

If you don't have a home computer you can get free access and help using the internet at your local library.

www.parentscentre.gov.uk
Comprehensive parenting website, including web-chats, interviews and videos.

www.parentlineplus.org.uk
Fantastic site offering support for parents with regard to their own feelings and experiences and including confidential email support.
Area offices also host regular 'parents together' groups and workshops.

www.bullying.co.uk
Award-winning site set up by a mother and her son in 1999 as a result of their experience of school bullying. Clear and easy to use, including confidential email support.

www.youthaccess.org.uk
Site of the national organization for young people's information, advice, counselling and support services. Carries details of free youth counselling in different areas.

www.education-otherwise.org
Useful site about educating children at home. Includes several email groups for parents and children.

www.bbc.co.uk
Brilliant site with loads of information about all kinds of things, including home schooling.

www.dfes.gov.uk/bullying
Here you can download the latest major government survey carried out by ChildLine, 'Tackling bullying: listening to the views of children and young people'.

www.anti-bullyingalliance.org/journeys.htm
This is the 2005 report on bullying by the Children's Commissioner – 'Journeys – Children and young people talking about bullying'. It includes ten children's real-life experiences of bullying, with comments from the Commissioner.